THE FIRST EASTER
WHAT REALLY HAPPENED?

By the Same Author in This Series

H.J. RICHARDS

THE FIRST EASTER

WHAT REALLY HAPPENED?

TWENTY-THIRD PUBLICATIONS

Mystic, Connecticut

ACKNOWLEDGMENTS

The author and publisher would like to acknowledge their indebtedness for permission to reproduce copyright material as follows: from *The Resurrection of Jesus of Nazareth* by Willi Marxsen — Copyright ©1970 by SCM Press Ltd. Used by permission of Fortress Press.

Excerpts from *The Jerusalem Bible*, copyright ©1966 by Darton, Longman & Todd Ltd, and Doubleday & Company Inc. Reprinted by permission of the publisher. The author has felt free to depart from this on a few occasions for the sake of precision.

North American edition 1986
by Twenty-Third Publications
P.O. Box 180
Mystic, CT 06355
(203) 536-2611

Previously published in Great Britain 1983
by A. R. Mowbray & Co., Ltd.
St. Thomas House
Beckett Street
Oxford, England

Library of Congress Catalog Card Number 85-51494
ISBN 0-89622-282-9

Cover design by George Herrick
Edited and designed by Helen Coleman

To my students
whose relentless questions
forced me to write this book

From my teachers I learnt much,
from my colleagues more,
but it was from my students
that I learnt most of all

Talmud, Ta'an 7a

Preface

This book was first published in England by Collins (*Fontana Books*) in 1976. A revised edition came out as a *Fount Paperback* in 1980, and when that edition went out of print, it was issued as one of Mowbray's *Popular Christian Paperbacks* in 1983. I welcome the opportunity to introduce this 1986 revision to a wider readership in North America.

The gospel stories are today receiving a publicity they have not enjoyed for centuries. What the scholars have to say about Jesus' birth, about the miracles attributed to him, and above all about his resurrection is suddenly making the headlines, and is today as liable to be discussed by door-to-door salespeople as by professors, in bars and over coffee as much as in churches.

This is not because the scholars are beginning to say something new. What they are saying they have been saying for decades. But perhaps they are beginning to say it more clearly, and hedging it about with fewer reservations. In their view, the gospel stories of Jesus' birth and death, of his miracles and his resurrection, are to be interpreted not as if they were news reports of events that could be recorded and televised, but as poetic expressions of faith. This does not make the stories less true than they would have been, only true in a different way.

The protests against this interpretation of gospel stories have been strong and vocal. "This is not how our forebears understood the stories." Perhaps not. But to understand the stories literally is just as much an interpretation as to understand them symbolically. Which interpretation is right is to be determined not by shouting the loudest, but by producing evidence.

In this book I have tried to present some of this evidence, as the scholars see it. I make no claim that all the scholars I have consulted agree with one another over all details. But they do increasingly agree that a critical reading of the New Testament no longer allows us to interpret all its stories as literally as was once common. If this agreement of the scholars cannot be called a consensus, it is at least a trend. This trend I have tried faithfully to reflect in the pages that follow, in the conviction that it will give blessed relief to many more people than it will disturb.

Contents

Introduction

I believe in the resurrection of Jesus Christ. I want to state this at the beginning of this work so no one can mistake my meaning, or accuse me of disbelieving this central fact of the Christian faith.

I don't object to being told that my understanding of the resurrection is different from someone else's. I don't object to being asked, "Yes, but in what does the resurrection consist?" — because that is precisely the question this book is concerned with. But at the end of the day I wish to stand with St. Paul, who launched Christianity into a pagan world with the bold statement, "If Christ has not been raised, then our preaching is useless, and your believing it is useless" (1 Corinthians 15:14). If I did not make that statement my own, I could not write as a Christian.

What I do object to is the suggestion that in this book I am using resurrection-language without really believing in the resurrection at all. That is equivalent to saying, "Only my idea of resurrection is valid." This is a presumptuous presumption, if I may put it like that. The opinion of recent theologians is more varied than many would imagine. The purpose of this book is to make their thinking available to a wider public than it generally reaches. I am convinced that this can do nothing but good. It may help the faith of many to grow, as it is meant to, from childish naivete into adult understanding.

Of all the problems posed by the New Testament, those posed by the resurrection stories are the most acute. For in the minds of many people, the resurrection acts as a kind of safety harness. I have in mind those who, at the beginning of this century, grudgingly allowed scholars to turn their critical attention to the Old Testament, "as long as they don't touch the New Testament"; and then later reluctantly allowed them to trespass on the New Testament, "as long as they don't touch the miracles"; and later still under protest allowed the critics to make a new appraisal of the miracle stories, "as long as they don't touch the resurrection." The New Testament is the Old Testament's safety harness, and the resurrection is the safety harness for its miracles. Interfere with the resurrection, they seem to say, and we shall all be in trouble!

In a sense these people have been right. They were wise, after their own fashion, to put up such a strong resistance over every inch they were forced to cede. At least they were more logical, and certainly more perceptive, than the liberal scholars who were so enthusiastically engrossed with the scientific task in hand that they never bothered to consider the consequences. The conservatives knew that the critical approach to the Bible could not be confined to the Old Testament, nor the investigation of the New Testament avoid the miracle stories, nor a discussion of the miraculous exclude the resurrection. Anyone who fears the journey's end should never start on this particular journey. It is naive to forbid awkward questions on the resurrection once they have been posed. Far better scotch the questions at root, and forbid scholars to meddle with the scriptures at all. Indeed this has been the declared policy of fundamentalists during every age of the Church's history.

But of course these people have also been profoundly wrong. Their attitude, for all its logic, is based on the assumption that critical research erodes people's faith. Certainly, if it does, one would have to ask what sort of faith these people had. But it is sheer silliness to make bogeymen of all scholars, and to imagine that they are either agents of Satan infiltrated into the Church to undermine its faith from within, or at best deluded fools who do not know the damage they are doing.

Of course, the demands that scholarship has made on the Christian community have always been painful. To reassess one's past understanding and reintegrate it into a new one is never easy. But the long-term result has always been an enrichment, never an impoverishment. Thanks to the work of scholars, the religious insights of the Old Testament can today be more readily appreciated than in the days when our only concern seemed to be to defend the historically and morally indefensible. The gospel too speaks more clearly, now that biblical theologians have helped us to distinguish between its timeless message and the time-bound context in which it was written. The New Testament miracles, perhaps for the first time in years, are again taken seriously by secularized readers whom the exegesis of experts has taught to ask questions appropriate to the stories and relevant to their lives. Finally our own decade, which has seen more scholarly work devoted to the resurrection than any other age in the Church's history, has allowed a "remythologization" which has liberated many who, without it, might have felt compelled to abandon their Christian faith.

The word "demythologization" is in vogue. For many people it has a sinister ring. They associate it with watering down and debunking. They could never use the word "myth" of the resurrection because that for them would put it in the realm of fairy stories and fantasy. "The resurrection is not a myth, it was an event," they say.

They need to be reassured. To call something a myth is not to dismiss it as a legend. There is nothing more real, or more true, than a myth. Myths are in fact what we live by. They are the symbols in which we express our deepest insights about ourselves and our universe. They are the poetry in which we express what we are and what we hold most dearly. The truths we live by, the values on which we base our lives — these can only be expressed inadequately, and in an indirect and symbolic way. Our most profound hopes and fears, the things we most yearn for and the things we most dread, our attitude to the ultimates in our lives — God and the world, life and death — these are not subject to mere logic and scientific analysis. They cannot be spoken of except obscurely through the medium of myth. "Myth is a way of telling the truth about the world we live in" (James P. Mackey, *Jesus, the Man and the Myth*, SCM, London, 1979, p. 121).

3

This means that no one can ever "demythologize" *tout court*, as if the reality embodied in the myth can be held or expressed "neat." All that a "demythologizer" can do is to make sure that the myth is recognized *as* myth, and not mistaken for a pedestrian scientific description. But what the myth speaks of will always need to be fleshed out in one form or another, and any attempt to "take off the wrapping" necessarily entails providing another one so that the mystery can be handled.

"Demythologization" therefore would more accurately be spoken of as "remythologization." Only it is important that the truths we live by should be expressed in a myth which is meaningful to us. To continue to express them in a myth which has gone dead on us means that the reality itself is in danger of dying on us.

That is why scholars have recently been turning their attention to the resurrection. It did not occur to past generations of Christians to ask awkward questions about the traditional stories of an empty tomb and a dead man coming back to life to walk and talk with his friends. The stories "found" them where they were, and spoke deeply to them. The Christian of today is not always in that situation. The secularized world in which this Christian has grown up, and the world-view he or she has inherited, seem to relegate the resurrection stories to a never-never land which has nothing to do with everyday life. Does there need to be this dichotomy between faith and living? Is it possible to express the meaning of the resurrection in terms of the world as the Christian knows it, not of some other world?

What is the resurrection concerned with anyway? What is the underlying reality to which it refers? To say that the resurrection is real does not say enough. The question is, What sort of reality are we dealing with? What exactly do Christians commit themselves to when saying of Jesus that "on the third day he rose again from the dead"? Can the underlying reality be remythologized, reformulated by us without our betraying the faith of those who handed it down to us?

These are the questions to which recent scholars have addressed themselves. This book presents their deliberation and conclusion. These may sound strange to those who are coming across them for the first time. I hasten to assure them that my purpose is not to shock or destroy, only to inform and build up. The questions which are being asked of the resurrection today may shatter some of our most treasured assumptions, but they can also lead us away from superficialities to the heart of the matter. Nor may we escape these awkward questions by dismissing those who pose them as "second-rate scholars": I have gone only to the most serious and respected, and wish only to act as their reporter and popularizer.

And if I am asked why I should wish to enter into such a controversial area, I can only reply in the words of G. K. Chesterton: "I believe in getting into hot water. I think it keeps you clean."

CHAPTER ONE

The Text

My five-year-old daughter recently had a nightmare. She awoke sobbing, and said she had dreamed that I was dead. I was able after much comforting to assure her that I wasn't, and she went back to bed. And back to her dream. She announced proudly next morning that the school secretary had put on a nurse's uniform, given me some medicine and wine, and I had got better.

The same week, the newspaper carried the striking headline, "Dead man recovers." An Irishman had walked across a frozen pond to rescue his dog, and had fallen through the ice. By the time he was rescued his body temperature was so low (10° C) that he was pronounced clinically dead. But in the hospital a heart surgeon familiar with hypothermia decided to operate in order to massage his heart. He revived and was able to leave the hospital within days (*The Times*, London, 29 March 1985).

I quote these two incidents in order to introduce a question we generally fight shy of: What sort of reality do we imagine resurrection to be? Is the "rising from the dead" to which Christians look forward the same kind of reality these incidents speak of, a wondrous coming back to life under the influence of some supernatural medicine, a divine message of hearts that have stopped? Whatever the answer, it will depend largely on our understanding of Jesus' resurrection. And since the only information that we have on this event (if information it is) is contained in the closing pages of the gospels and the opening paragraphs of the Acts, the texts must be examined and analysed.

AWKWARD QUESTIONS

The extent to which the stories of Jesus' resurrection bristle with difficulties is not generally appreciated. Most of those who come upon these stories in the closing pages of the gospel assume that they form one coherent picture, with one scene following another with perfect consistency. The naiveté of their view will become apparent to them as soon as they begin to ask a few questions.

In fact, anyone wishing to *feel* the problem personally rather than simply to read about it would do well to spread the various accounts out before him,[1] and compare them closely to see what answers they can provide to such questions as the following:

When exactly did the burial of Jesus take place?

John: the embalming is completed on the Friday night.

Luke: the spices are prepared on the Friday evening.

Mark: the spices are not bought till the Saturday evening.

How was the body buried?

Matthew: in a sealed and guarded tomb.

---

[1]The gospel texts are summarized, for convenience, in the tables on pp. 18ff. and 30ff.

7

Mark, Luke: unembalmed body in an unsealed tomb.

At what time on Sunday did the first witnesses come to the tomb?

John: while it was still dark.

Matthew, Luke: at dawn.

Mark: at sunrise.

Who were these witnesses?

Matthew: the two Maries.

Mark: the two Maries and Salome.

Luke: the two Maries, Joanna and others.

John: Mary of Magdala alone, (though she speaks in the plural).

How did they find the stone?

Matthew: being rolled back.

Mark, Luke, John: already rolled back.

What did they see there?

Matthew, Mark: one angel.

Luke, John: two angels.

Matthew: outside the tomb.

Mark, Luke, John: inside the tomb.

(*Luke, John*: Peter and John see no angels).

When did the women enter the tomb?

Mark, Luke: before the angelic message.

Matthew: after.

What was the message?

> *Luke, John*: the risen Jesus will shortly appear to the disciples.

> *Matthew, Mark*: he will not appear until later, in Galilee.

How did they react?

> *Mark*: with such fear that they told no one.

> *Matthew, Luke, John*: with such joy that they immediately told all the disciples.

Who was actually the first to see the risen Christ?

> *Matthew, John*: these women.

> *Luke*: Peter.

> (*Mark*: no appearance of Christ is mentioned).

Where did Christ make a public appearance to the disciples?

> *Luke, John*: in Jerusalem, with instructions not to leave there.

> *Matthew*: in Galilee, where they are told to go immediately.

How many public appearance were there?

> *Matthew, Luke*: one.

> *John*: two.

> *Acts, John's Appendix*: several.

What were the disciples told?

> *Matthew, Luke, John* have three different accounts.

Where did the last appearance take place?

> *Matthew*: in Galilee.

> *Luke*: in Jerusalem.

When did Jesus ascend to heaven?

Luke, John: on the same day as the appearances.

Acts: only after forty days.

When did the risen Christ "send" the Holy Spirit?

John: on Easter day.

Acts: only after fifty days.

"SAVING" THE STORIES

These questions are not posed to make fun of the text, only to discover its real purpose. There are some who naively imagine that, in spite of such questions, it is quite possible to make one coherent account of the resurrection stories.[1] They suggest that the "slight differences" are really a proof of authenticity, and that too much neat consistency between one evangelist and the next would arouse suspicion of collusion.

Such a solution is a desperate one. The fact is that, as literal descriptions of what took place, the stories are quite incoherent and totally irreconcilable. There were once very few New Testament scholars bold enough to say this. Today nearly all of them do, even the most conservative. Any attempt to "save" the stories by omitting details, or by twisting and bending them so that they will vaguely dovetail into each other, is clumsy and dishonest.

Does this mean that the stories should be rejected as worthless? How extraordinary that some people should come to such an extreme conclusion. Surely the more obvious inference is that the stories were never intended as literal descriptions of a sequence of events, and should not be treated as such.

Is it not worth remarking that the evangelists themselves seem to show little interest in achieving the kind of consistency that we keep looking for? Faced with the inconsistencies revealed by the questions we were asking above — and they must have been aware of some of them at least — the

---

[1] One of the most recent attempts is by J. Wenham in *Easter Enigma* (*Devon, England: Paternoster Press Ltd.*, 1984).

10

evangelists did not bat an eyelid. They did not seem to consider them important.

LOOKING CLOSER

Let us look again, and more closely, at a detail already referred to above. Mark's gospel (omitting the appendix, see note on p. 19) is able to speak of the resurrection without describing any appearance of the risen Christ at all. The only appearance referred to is spoken of as eventually due to take place in Galilee; in Jerusalem there is nothing for the disciples but the message to proceed to Galilee according to the arrangements Jesus made with them before he died.

Yet Luke, writing his gospel with this page of Mark open before him (it was one of his sources), not only places all the appearances of Jesus in Jerusalem, but explicitly excludes Galilee: the disciples are to remain in Jerusalem until Pentecost (Luke 24:49).

To take another example. All the gospel accounts speak of the resurrection in terms of an empty tomb. Whether it is Matthew writing or Mark, Luke or John, all four seem to want to focus the reader's attention on the grave in Jerusalem which was found empty on Easter morning. Yet, in spite of this, the many references to the resurrection in the epistles of Paul do not have the slightest hint of an empty tomb. Now, Paul's epistles may be considered either as earlier than the gospels or as later than them; most of them were written before the present gospels, though the preaching now embodied in the gospels was current before Paul wrote. In either case, the discrepancy is remarkable. Paul even speaks of an appearance of the risen Christ years after the ascension which, according to the gospel account, marked the end of the appearances.

In short, when the text is looked at closely, it would seem that the resurrection and ascension of Jesus, whatever it actually consisted of, was not dependent on the appearance of Jesus, or on an empty tomb, or on a specific place, or on a specific time. Different New Testament writers speak of the reality that stands behind Jesus' resurrection and ascension in different ways: in terms of appearances or non-appearances, in terms of Jerusalem or Galilee, as involving an empty tomb or a full one, as extending over a period of forty days or of one. There is no *one* coherent or consistent or exclusive account of the resurrection of Jesus. There are many ways in which the reality of the risen and ascended Christ can be expressed. Why should this be so?

Because the stories in which this reality was conveyed were not meant to be taken as word-for-word descriptions, in the way that stories in a biography might be. In their different ways, they were simply intended as concrete expressions of what the experience of the resurrection meant to those who told the stories. The stories speak *as if* the event was visible and tangible, audible and measurable — but this is only a way of insisting that the experience underlying them is a real one, not an imaginary one. It took place in the objective world, not merely in people's minds. The fact nonetheless remains that one story can be quite inconsistent with the next *as story*. This did not matter to those who told or wrote the stories. The important thing was that the stories expressed the same *faith*. The stories remain free and independent of each other because each is only a vehicle of faith, not the basis of faith. Faith is based, as always, on a personal meeting with the risen Christ.

THE LITERARY FORM OF THE GOSPEL

One of the reasons we find it difficult to approach the resurrection stories in this way is that we are not sufficiently alive to the kind of literature that the gospels really are. They look like biography, and so we tend to read them as biography. Because the evangelists have joined one story to the next with the link-words "then, next, afterwards," we are tempted to read the text as a literal description of a sequence of events.

We need to remind ourselves, and often, that not one of these stories was written or even preached before the disciples believed in the resurrection. Each was composed by believing Christians for believing Christians. For both, Jesus was no longer simply a figure from the past, but a living person whom writer and reader had met and continued to meet as the risen Lord. No one could write of what such a person said and did twenty, thirty or fifty years before, and think he was merely composing a chronicle. Whatever he wrote, it would always be a presentation of that risen Lord, a making present of that Christ who lives on into the present. In short, all the gospel stories are resurrection stories, influenced by the resurrection event and expressing the resurrection faith.

But if that is true of the gospel stories in general, it must be true above all of the resurrection stories. It would be absurd to accept all the New Testament stories as expressions of faith in the risen Christ *except* the resurrection stories themselves, and to take these as word-for-word descriptions of what happened. No, the stories about the resurrection were also told by and for people who had experienced Christ as a person living on into the present, and the stories were meant to recapture that experience. The resurrection stories, like the other gospel stories, were never meant to be read as simple biography. They were meant to be a profession of faith. They were attempts to express in a concrete way what the risen Christ meant, here and now, to the believer. The stories were moulded by the faith of those who told them. They had little or no meaning for those who did not share that faith. They were spoken from faith, to faith.

CRUDE LITERALISM

It seems to me important to present the resurrection stories in this light, lest we place an unnecessary obstacle in people's path. If a piece of writing is designed as an invitation to faith, then to present it as a piece of information or literal description may prevent the reader from ever coming to faith.

A crude and literalist understanding of the word "resurrection" would take Ezekiel's brilliant poetic image of the Valley of Dry Bones (Ezekiel 37) and open it out as the negro spiritual does, with the appropriate jangle of bone against bone to punctuate the music.

> Just connect them bones, them dry bones . . .
> When the head bone's connected to the neck bone . . .
> The back bone's connected to the hip bone . . .
> The thigh bone's connected to the leg bone . . . (etc.)

> Now hear the word of the Lord:
> Them bones, them bones gonna rise again,
> Them bones, them bones gonna walk around . . .
> Now hear the word of the Lord!

The extent to which this kind of "resurrection" corresponds to the thinking of many people was illustrated by a presentation of Christianity in a French television series. It was phenomenally successful, in spite of the fact that it spoke of Jesus' death and resurrection with almost unbelievable crudity in the following terms (my italics):

> Catholic dogma states that Jesus, who forms part of God since he is one of the three aspects of the Holy Trinity (Father, Son and Holy Ghost), came to this earth to become man, lived a truly human life, suffered a really human death, but *three days later, by means of his divine nature, revivified his corpse which had momentarily been inactive,* and finally disappeared into the inaccessible regions where the divinity resides. He will come back from there at the Last Judgement to bring about a general resurrection of all men's corpses, so that they can live with him for ever. . . .

Christianity states that the divine is geared into the ordinary everyday human world, the clutch-peddle being Jesus' incarnation into the body of a man, *and subsequently his death and resurrection.* God connected with the world by sending Jesus. *When Jesus died he disengaged.* But there had been a short contact between God and the world, between motor and transmission, and the world was propelled forward by the impetus given to it while the clutch-peddle was engaged (Roger Mauge, *Jesus,* Paris 1971, pp. 318, 321).

A WORLD-VIEW

Perhaps those who feel at home in that kind of world should be left undisturbed in it. But they ought in charity to realize that some people today — and their number is growing — can no longer live with that sort of world-view, or with the God it presupposes, however great its success on television. Bishop John Robinson accurately caught the mood of these people in the title of his paperback, *But That I Can't Believe!* Today more and more people are asking whether Christianity ties them down to such a literalistic — indeed materialistic — view of their relationship with God, and whether it is not possible —without any watering down — to express what God has done for them in Christ in other terms.

Certainly a materialistic concept of resurrection does not strike many people today as gospel or good news. Going by their own experience, they think of the body as a prison, a barrier to communication. To tell them that they are going to be encumbered with that for all eternity will destroy their hope of eternal life, not build it up. Is this the only way in which we can speak of the resurrection of the body, whether of Christ or of ourselves?

Those who insist on interpreting Jesus' resurrection as his physical restoration have perhaps never considered the difficulties raised by such a view. How, for instance, do they cope with the idea of the corpse of someone who has died a violent death with all the accompanying loss of blood and damage to brain, heart and cells? Do they presume that there was a massive divine intervention to repair all this damage by miracle? What do they make of a revivified corpse which was 'objectively' seen by Peter and Cleopas, and which might therefore just as easily have been seen by Pilate and Caiaphas? When did it not appear much more convincingly to them anyway? And where was it in between the appearances? What was the miraculously reconstituted corpse dressed in — miraculous clothes? Or was it naked (this has actually been suggested as the reason for the words addressed to the Magdalene, "Do not touch me!")?

What do they make of such a corpse-come-back-to-life ascending to heaven? Are the molecules and cells of that body somewhere in our universe — and if so where? On a star? Etherealized into energy waves? (This has actually been suggested.) But do we really need to resort to fantasies of this kind to state where the risen Christ is now?

The more seriously we adopt a world-view in which

reality is to be explained in terms of the world we know and have experienced, and not in terms of invisible forces intervening from a second world outside, the more we are forced to ask ourselves: What does the resurrection of Jesus mean in secular language? What is the reality behind the religious and symbolic language in which we usually describe it? Is two-world language the only language in which to speak of the resurrection?

THE HEART OF THE MATTER

We are led back, inevitably, to the heart of the matter. At the core of the gospel stands the message of "incarnation," the good news that God is operative in human history, that is to say, in a history like the one we have known and experienced, not in some never-never land or in some fairy-like "once-upon-a-time." This is the distinctive contribution that Judaeo-Christianity has to make to man's understanding of himself. History, our history, is God-filled. If we keep decorating this God-filled history with stories which, taken as literal description, make it quite unlike our own history, then we have obscured the gospel's central message. We have distorted its meaning because we are no longer taking "incarnation" seriously.

This emphasis on the incarnational manner of God's relationship with man is to be found in much recent theological writing. Scripture scholar Raymond Brown writes of the Virgin Birth in words that would apply equally to the gospel miracles and to the gospel narratives of the resurrection:

> Inevitably, no matter how hard one may try to be objective in such an inquiry, there are certain predispositions towards a particular solution. In times past the predispositions would have been favourable towards the historicity of the virginal conception [or the miraculous, or the literal understanding of the resurrection narratives]. It was expected that the marvellous should accompany God's actions among men, and the miraculous supported faith. In recent times, however, the miraculous has created suspicion among many Chris-

16

tians. This is more than mere rationalism or the association of the miraculous with the credulous. Rather it stems from an appreciation of what is truly unique in the Judaeo-Christian religion, namely, a conviction that God has been operative in human history, a history like our own. A history studded with the miraculous is not the history we live in. And so recent predispositions have run against the thesis that Jesus, who was like us in all but sin, should have been conceived differently from other men [or possessed of powers quite unlike ours, or enjoyed a post-mortem existence beyond our possibilities] (*The Virginal Conception and Bodily Resurrection of Jesus*, Chapman, London 1973, p 29).

But it is time to discuss, more closely, the *stories* in which the evangelists expressed their faith (chapter 2), and the deeper *reality* those stories were intended to convey (chapter 3).

The Story

To allow the reader to make some kind of assessment of the resurrection story, I thought it useful to paraphrase. And rather than print out the various gospel accounts in sequence, I have tabulated them so that the reader can compare them and see at a glance the similarities and differences.

THE EMPTY TOMB STORIES

MATTHEW	MARK
Joseph of Arimathea, a disciple of Jesus, asks Pilate for Jesus's body,	Joseph of Arimathea asks Pilate for Jesus' body,

The stories of the empty tomb are immediately below, those of the resurrection appearances on p. 30ff. In the latter case, I have listed the appendices to the gospels of Mark and John separately because scholars are agreed that, important though they are, they did not form part of these gospels as originally planned. Mark's appendix in fact is clearly dependent on Luke and John.

LUKE	JOHN
Joseph of Arimathea	Joseph of Arimathea,
	a hidden disciple of Jesus,
asks Pilate for Jesus' body,	asks Pilate for Jesus's body.

MATTHEW	MARK
wraps it in a clean shroud, and places it in his own new rock-cut tomb. The tomb is closed with a large rolling stone, witnessed by	wraps it in a shroud, and places it in a rock-cut tomb. The tomb is closed with a rolling stone, witnessed by
Mary of Magdala	Mary of Magdala
and the other Mary.	and Mary mother of Joset.
After Preparation Day, the priests and Pharisees, anticipating a stolen body and a claim of resurrection, ask for a guard for three days. Pilate grants this, and the tombstone is sealed.	
On the Sunday, Mary of Magdala and the other Mary	On the Sunday, Mary of Magdala, Mary mother of James, and Salome buy spices
go to the tomb at dawn.	and go to the tomb after sunrise.
	"Who will roll away the stone?"
An earthquake. The stone is moved by the Angel in white, who sits on it. The guards are terrified. The Angel says, "Do not fear.	They find the stone rolled back. They enter the tomb, and see a young man in white sitting on the right. They are terrified. He says, "Do not fear.

20

LUKE	JOHN
	Joseph and Nicodemus
wraps it in a shroud,	wrap it in linen cloths,
and places it	and place it
in a new rock-cut tomb,	in a new tomb in a nearby
	garden
witnessed by the women	
who had come from Galilee,	
(Mary of Magdala,	
Joanna,	
Mary mother of James	
and others)	
who then go to prepare spices.	after embalming it with spices.
On the Sunday,	On the Sunday,
	Mary of Magdala
they take the prepared spices	
and go to the tomb	goes to the tomb
very early.	while it is still dark.
They find the stone rolled back.	She finds the stone moved.
They enter	Later she looks inside the tomb,
and see two men in white.	and sees two angels in white
	seated.
They say,	They say,
	"Why do you weep?"

21

MATTHEW	MARK
You are looking for Jesus crucified.	You are looking for Jesus crucified. He has been raised. He is not here.
He is not here. He has been raised. See the place where they put him. Tell the disciples, He is going before you to Galilee. You will see him there."	See the place where they put him. Tell the disciples and Peter, He is going before you to Galilee. You will see him there."
They leave the tomb in fear and joy, and tell the disciples.	They leave the tomb in fear and terror, and tell no one.

LUKE	JOHN
"Why look	She says,
for the living among the dead? He is not here. He has been raised.	"They have taken away my Lord, I don't know where they have put him."
Remember that he told you	
in Galilee	
that he would be raised on the third day."	
They leave the tomb,	
and tell the Eleven	She tells the disciples "I have seen the Lord."
and all the others, who disbelieve them.	
	Mary of Magdala tells Simon Peter and the disciple Jesus loved, "They have taken the Lord from the tomb. We don't know where they have put him."
Peter runs to the tomb,	Peter and the other run to the tomb.
looks in, and sees the cloths,	The other disciple looks in, and sees the cloths. Peter arrives and enters and sees the cloths and head- cloth. The other disciple enters and believes.

23

MATTHEW   MARK

The guards tell the high priests,
        what happened.
    They are bribed to say
that the disciples stole the body,
        while they slept.
    The guards take the bribe
        and spread this story
        up till the present.

A TOMB NOT FOUND EMPTY

The exhibition of Tutankhamun's treasures, recently mounted
in many of the world's capitals, aroused great interest in the
story of the original discovery of those treasures fifty years ago
by the British archaeologist Dr. Howard Carter. A recording
of Carter's own description of that discovery was re-issued, in
which he said:

> I suppose most excavators would confess to a feeling of
> awe, almost embarrassment, when they break into a
> tomb closed and sealed by pious hands so many centur-
> ies ago. Thirty-three centuries had passed since human
> feet last trod the floor on which we stood, and yet the
> signs of recent life were around us: a half-filled bowl of
> mortar, a blackened lamp, the chips of wood left on the
> floor by a careless carpenter.
>
> We had penetrated two chambers, but when we
> came to a golden shrine with doors closed and sealed,

LUKE	JOHN
and goes home amazed.	They go home.

"Some women went to the tomb
early in the morning,
and not finding the body,
came back with the angels'
message
that he was alive.
The disciples checked the tomb
and could not find him."

---

we realized that we were in the presence of the dead king. We were to witness a spectacle such as no other man in our time had been privileged to see.

I carefully cut the cord, removed the precious seal, drew back the bolts and opened the doors: when a second shrine was revealed, even more brilliant in workmanship than the last.

With intense excitement I went forward and unbolted the inner doors. They slowly swung open, and there, filling the entire area within, stood an immense yellow quartzite sarcophagus. It effectively barred any further progress until we could raise the lid. Then a decisive moment. None of us but felt the solemnity of the occasion. In a dead silence the huge lid, weighing over a ton and a quarter, was raised from its bed. Light shone into the sarcophagus. But how disappointing: the contents were completely covered by linen shrouds. But as the last shroud was rolled back, a gasp of wonderment escaped our lips, so gorgeous was the sight that met our eyes.

A golden effigy of the young king, of magnificent workmanship, filled the whole of the interior. This was but the lid of a series of three coffins nested one within the other, enclosing the mortal remains of the young king Tutankhamun.

Laid on that golden outer lid was a tiny wreath of flowers, as it pleased us to think, the last farewell offering of the widowed girl-queen to her husband. Among all that regal splendour, everywhere the glint of gold, there was nothing so beautiful as those few withered flowers. They told us what a short period 3,300 years really was: but yesterday and the morrow. (BBC Sound Archives Recording, REB 78 M)

WHAT SORT OF STORY?

Carter tells his story well, with a fine eye for colorful detail and an arresting use of suspense. But then so did the evangelists. If one was asked the principal difference between the two stories, one might be excused for pointing to the fact that in one story the tomb was empty, and in the other it was not. But the real difference lies much deeper.

Of its nature, Carter's story is a chronicle. He is describing an actual event, and rehearsing in historical terms what he physically saw, heard and touched. The literary form he uses to tell his story is history.

Of its nature, the gospel story is something other than that. The evangelists had no intention of writing a simple chronicle. They wanted to express their faith in a Christ whose mode of existence has nothing to do with what can be seen by looking into tombs. The literary form they used to tell their story is gospel, or profession of faith.

In other words, both Howard Carter and the evangelists tell a story. At first sight the two seem comparable: they are both on the same subject. In fact the two stories serve an entirely different purpose, and one cannot be compared with the other. In one case the story is meant to convey information, in the other to evoke the reader's faith. The first story demands accuracy, consistency and coherence. The other does not, and we have already seen in the analysis of the text that it does not provide this. This would be surprising only if it purported to be a descriptive story of the first kind. It clearly does not.

THE EMPTY TOMB AS PROOF

For all the emphasis placed on it, the empty tomb is a very ambiguous element in the resurrection story. After all, there are more ways than one of emptying a tomb. There is always the possibility of grave-robbing by people who have something to make out of it. Howard Carter's discovery of Tutankhamun's tomb intact is unique precisely because the tombs of the other pharaohs had all been robbed ages before. And robbery by the disciples is the first possibility offered for consideration in the story as told by Matthew — even though he goes on to reject it. But it was not only the disciples of Jesus who might have been interested in abducting Jesus' corpse; his enemies too would have an interest in such a project, in order to foil the disciples. One could even envisage people finding a tomb empty because they were looking in the wrong tomb.

I am not trying to suggest that it was one of these things — grave robbery or mistaken identity — that actually happened. I am simply saying that if the empty tomb is such an ambiguous element in the story, it cannot be made into the main platform of an argument. No one could base his faith in Jesus' resurrection on the empty tomb alone. An empty tomb, of itself, cannot prove anything.

THE EMPTY TOMB AS SYMBOL

It is interesting, therefore, that in the story itself the empty tomb alone convinces no one. When the apostles are first told of it in Luke's account, it is quite insufficient to bring them to faith. Even the Magdalene of the story can only come to the conclusion, "They have taken my Lord away, I don't know where." No one speaks resurrection-language, or says, "I believe in the resurrection" until they have seen Jesus himself.

27

In this context, it is worth repeating that in the first preaching of the resurrection the empty tomb played no part. There is no whisper of an empty tomb in any of Paul's writings, or in the sermons in Acts 2, 3, 4, 5, 10 and 13. Of "seeing" the risen Christ, yes; this is what convinced Paul and others that Jesus was indeed raised from the dead. But he makes no reference anywhere to a tomb being emptied, whether miraculously or otherwise, even when he is only quoting the Easter faith handed on to him. In fact, given his understanding of resurrection, he would have found an empty tomb a distinct embarrassment.

An empty tomb would demand the resuscitation of a corpse, or of what Paul calls a "body of the flesh," whereas the resurrection has to do with a "body of the spirit." Here is what Paul has to say about the two:

> Whatever you sow in the ground
> has to die before it is given new life
> and the thing that you sow
> is not what is going to come . . .
> The thing that is sown is perishable
> but what is raised is imperishable;
> the thing that is sown is contemptible
> but what is raised is glorious;
> the thing that is sown is weak
> but what is raised is powerful;
> when it is sown it embodies the soul,
> when it is raised it embodies the spirit.
> If the soul has its own embodiment,
> so does the spirit have its own embodiment . . .
> Flesh and blood cannot inherit the kingdom of God:
> and the perishable cannot inherit what lasts for ever.
> (1 Corinthians 15:36–50)

In other words, the risen body is not just the physical body etherealized. It exists in a completely different order of reality. A "body of spirit" has nothing to do with dead bones, or with eating, or with being touched. It is a body transposed into a new order of being, where walking or eating or touching simply do not apply. The reality of resurrection has nothing to do with bringing the physical "body of the flesh" back to life.

This leads many scholars to suggest that the "empty tomb" is simply a symbol. Even the moderate C. H. Dodd asks: "Is it possible that the earliest Christians, convinced on other grounds that Jesus was still alive, gave expression to this conviction in an imaginative or symbolic form suggested by the common belief (in life after death as a kind of resuscitation of the body which was buried), and that this was the origin of the story in the gospels? It may be so" (*The Founder of Christianity*, Collins, London 1971, p.166f.).

A parallel may illustrate the point. The phrase in John's gospel, "The doors were closed but Jesus came in" (20:26) does not mean that Jesus entered literally through the wall. Why should he begin his appearance outside the room instead of more conveniently inside? The phrase is merely a vivid way of saying that he does not need to enter because he is already present in the community.

Likewise the empty tomb could be simply a pictorial image of the fact that, after Easter, Jesus is no longer among the dead. The cemetery is not the place where you should look for him. Even though all four gospels use this image, implying that the tradition about the empty tomb is an extremely venerable one, there is no reason why it should be anything more than a concrete way of expressing the conviction that Jesus now lives a new kind of life, where there is no more death. Death could not hold him prisoner. He is not to be found by searching in a graveyard.

Certainly a literally empty tomb is not crucial to faith in resurrection which does not depend on the reanimation of a corpse; indeed anyone believing in his own future resurrection has to make this part of his faith. Less still does resurrection *consist* of the reanimation of a corpse: it is a different sort of reality altogether, which we shall analyse more closely below. Christian faith does not stand or fall on the story of the empty tomb, but on the conviction that Jesus is alive. Raymond Brown puts it succinctly: "Christians believe in Jesus, not in a tomb" (*op. cit.,* p. 127).

29

THE APPEARANCE STORIES

MATTHEW	LUKE

The women returning from the
tomb
meet Jesus.

(They do not recognize him
24:16)

He greets them.

They fall down and clasp his
feet.
Jesus says, "Do not be afraid.

Tell my brothers
to go to Galilee

There they will see me."

Two disciples
on their way to Emmaus,
reflecting on the death of Jesus,
are joined by Jesus

They do not recognize him.
Cleopas explains their dismay.
"They crucified him.
We had hoped he would deliver
Israel.
A story that he is alive.
He has disappeared."
Jesus explains the scriptures
that the Messiah must enter
glory
through suffering.

30

APPENDIX MARK 16:9-20	JOHN
Mary of Magdala	Mary of Magdala turns
sees him first.	and sees Jesus standing there, but does not recognize him, supposing him to be the gardener. Jesus says, "Mary." Mary says, "Rabbuni, Master." Jesus says, "Do not cling to me,
	I have not yet ascended.
	Tell the brothers, 'I am ascending to the Father.'"
She tells the disciples,	She tells the disciples, "I have seen the Lord."
who refuse to believe her.	
Two disciples on a country road	
see him under another form.	

MATTHEW   LUKE

He stays with them
and breaks bread for them.
They recognize him,
but he vanishes.
They return to tell the Eleven

to be told that
Jesus has appeared to Simon.

On Easter day
Jesus stands among the disciples
and says "Peace."
They think it is a ghost.
"Why are you upset?
See my hands
and my feet.
It is me.
Touch and see:
a ghost has no flesh and bones."
They cannot believe it
for joy.
"Have you something to eat?"
They give him fish.
He eats it before them.

He explains the scriptures
that the Messiah must suffer
and rise.
Forgiveness must be preached
to all
beginning from Jerusalem.
"Stay there awaiting
the Father's promised Spirit."

APPENDIX MARK 16:9-20   APPENDIX JOHN 21

(Jesus takes bread and gives it
to them 21:13)

They tell the others
who refuse to believe.

JOHN

On Easter day
Jesus stands among the disciples
and says "Peace."

Jesus appears to the Eleven

and reproaches their unbelief

He shows them his hands
and his side.

They rejoice to see the Lord.

at table.

"I send you as I was sent.

Sins you forgive are forgiven

Receive the Holy Spirit."
Thomas refuses to believe
that they have seen the Lord
"unless I touch him."

MATTHEW   LUKE

The Eleven go to Galilee
to the appointed mountain.
They see Jesus and adore,
though some hesitate.
Jesus says,
"All authority is mine.
Go and make disciples everywhere,
and baptize them.

Teach them what I have taught
you.
I shall be with you always."

APPENDIX MARK 16-9-20

JOHN

A week later
Jesus stands among them
and says, "Peace.
Put your finger in my hands
and your hand into my side,
and believe."
"My Lord and my God."
"Blessed are those who have not
seen."

Jesus says,

"Go out to the whole world

He who believes and is baptized
will be saved.
Proclaim the Good News to all."

Signs associated with believers.

APPENDIX JOHN 21

Jesus appears by Tiberias
to Simon Peter,
Thomas, Nathanael,
John and James,
and two others.
They have been fishing at night
and caught nothing.
At daylight,
Jesus stands on the shore
unrecognized.
"Throw the net to starboard."
They cannot haul the large catch.
The disciple Jesus loved says,
"It is the Lord."
Simon Peter jumps into the water.
The others tow the net to land.
"Bring some of the 153 fish,

MATTHEW   LUKE

Jesus leads them towards
Bethany,
blesses them,
withdraws,
and is carried up to heaven.
They return to Jerusalem
with joy.

WHAT SORT OF STORIES?

What sort of stories are these? From the earliest times there
have been suggestions that the appearances spoken of in these
texts were entirely subjective, that is to say, self-induced delu-
sions. The community of disciples, shaken to the roots by the
events of Good Friday, haunted by memories of Jesus and
unable to accept the fact of his death, would have begun to
imagine that he was still alive. The appearances would be
simply the result of their own wishful thinking. They believed
in his resurrection because they wanted to, or because they
expected it.

One could accept this as a possible explanation of the
appearance stories if they told of only one appearance to one
person. A single person might possibly have woven an appearance of the risen Christ out of his imagination. But the stories

36

APPENDIX MARK 16-9-20   APPENDIX JOHN 21

and have breakfast."
No one asks, Who are you,
knowing it is the Lord.
Jesus takes bread
and gives it to them
with the fish.

After speaking to them

Jesus is taken up into heaven.

---

tell of repeated appearances to many individuals, even to groups, even to crowds; and however difficult it may be to reconcile the stories, they do not give the impression of a wish-projection supported by mass hysteria. It is more reasonable to assume that the stories arose because *something* happened.

What exactly? If "something entirely subjective" is ruled out, is the only alternative "something entirely objective," that is to say, something that could have been photographed and tape-recorded? The stories as they stand do not easily accord with this explanation either.

SUBJECTIVE OR OBJECTIVE?

To begin with, many of the stories make a feature of the difficulty the visionaries have in recognizing the appearances for what they are. The Magdalene thinks she is seeing the gardener (John); the couple at Emmaus converse with their "vision" for some time before they realize who it is (Luke); the disciples do not dare ask "Who are you?" since they know quite well (!) who it is (John's appendix); some disciples are hesitant about falling down before the risen Jesus (Matthew); and Jesus reproaches them for their doubts (Luke, Mark's appendix). In other words, the "apparition," whatever it is, is not immediately recognizable. And when it is recognized for the risen Christ, it is not because Christ has taken off a mask. It is the disciples who have changed, not he.

Secondly (and I have already mentioned this), it is significant that the appearances are restricted to believers. The stories do not tell of any "impartial" non-believers being included among the visionaries — Herod, Caiaphas, Pilate —however much more impressive their evidence would have been. Whatever it is that is "seen," it is apparently accessible only to believers.

Thirdly, the conclusion of each vision is not "We have seen Jesus," but "We have seen the Lord." This is a theological statement, expressing not a mere physical sight but an insight. These visionaries had "seen" that Jesus had entered the realm of "the Lord," or of God.

Finally, it is interesting to note that if the stories are detached from their context and read individually, each can be understood as describing a first appearance of the risen Lord. Each is said to take the viewer completely by surprise. When Paul tries to sum up the evidence he produces the list of appearances in 1 Corinthians 15:5-8. But the gospel stories do not read like a sequence of events; one appearance does not necessarily come after or depend on the one that went before. Each is a first. Each is a separate "coming to see" what the resurrection is about.

All this suggests that the resurrection is the kind of reality which cannot be classified under the category of "subjective'" or "objective," as if it were just like other events in space and time. Certainly the appearances were not merely "subjective" in the sense of imaginary or purely internal. But neither were they simply "objective" in the sense of physical and available to all onlookers. They belong to a different category, the category of faith. Faith is indeed a subjective operation in the sense that the believer must do his own believing; no one else can do it for him. But he believes in something more than his own experience. He knows that what he believes in exists independently of himself.

The stories of the appearances of Jesus, even more than those of the empty tomb, are symbols. They are a pictorial and concrete way of expressing faith in the risen Christ. In story form, that faith can only be expressed in the words, "I have seen the Lord." Outside of such a story, the believer can only say, "I believe in the risen Christ."

WHICH CAME FIRST?

The extent to which these stories are symbolic rather than descriptive can be gauged from the fact that none of them, even the earliest, attempts to deal with the event which is presupposed to lie behind them all: the actual raising of Jesus from the tomb.[1] They all begin with events which, in the story, are subsequent to that, namely the discovery of the tomb or the appearance of the risen Christ. The stories tell of the consequences of resurrection, not of resurrection itself. They state that what people "saw" was not the raising from the dead but the risen Christ. What came first was the experience of meeting the risen Christ, and the description followed.

In other words, it was not the events spoken of in the stories which convinced people that Jesus was alive. It was exactly the other way round: it was people's conviction that Jesus was raised from the dead that gave rise to the stories. What came first was the message, "Jesus is alive," and the narrative came afterwards.

---

[1] The apocryphal *Gospel of Peter*, dating from the second century AD, describes two men coming down from heaven and entering the tomb to lead forth a third "whose head was higher than the heavens," the procession being brought up by a cross which speaks; but none of the canonical gospels dares to use language as pictorial as this.

This can be corroborated by simply putting the stories into the chronological order in which they were composed. The earliest of them have the fewest details; they only become more concrete and more detailed as time goes on. In the 50s and 60s, Paul says simply that the risen Christ appeared to him, and Mark is able to convey the reality of the resurrection without mentioning any appearance at all. In the 70s, Matthew speaks of the risen Christ delivering a discourse to his disciples. By the 80s, Luke tells the story of a Christ who holds a conversation with his disciples, explains the scriptures to them, and then sits down to eat a meal with them. In the 90s, the Christ of John's gospel shows the disciples his wounded hands and side, and bids the doubting Thomas feel them with his finger and his hands. The final addition to John's gospel presents a Christ who makes a fire and cooks breakfast for his disciples. Clearly, stories which grow like this in the telling need to be taken *as* stories, not as history.

HOW EVENT BECAME NARRATIVE

What gave rise to these stories? What went into the making of them? How did the original event turn into narrative? New Testament scholars suggest several factors.

There is first the element of dramatization, the need to express in a concrete and pictorial form a mystery which would otherwise remain almost inexpressible. The "discourses" of the risen Christ, for instance, differing as they do from one gospel to the next, are clear examples of the way in which some of the implications of Jesus' teaching were opened out in the light of the disciples' Easter experience. But such a realization, involving as it did a complete reinterpretation of the Old Testament, could not, in the nature of things, come to the apostles out of the blue. They needed time to arrive at this new understanding of the scriptures, and to assess what the risen Christ demanded of them. The Christ of the resurrection did indeed give them their missionary mandate, but only through their own gradual understanding of what his teaching, his life and his death implied.

The story of the doubting Thomas is also recognized by scholars to be a piece of dramatization. I have already pointed out that all the evangelists mention fear and disbelief as one of the apostles' first reactions to their encounter with the risen Christ. John has decided to dramatize this, to highlight this attitude by focusing it on to one person. His efforts were highly successful: his story has remained embedded in the minds of most Christians who are unaware that the other evangelists had all said the same thing less dramatically. "Such free dramatization is characteristic of the Fourth Gospel," says Raymond Brown after his exhaustive study of John (*op. cit.*, p. 106, f.n. 176).

A second element which contributed towards the making of the stories is consistency. Once anyone commits himself to expressing his faith in a story rather than in abstract statements, the story is inevitably going to take over. The result is, if an objection to the story is raised, he cannot reply, "But the story is only expressing my faith." The logic of the situation demands that he elaborate the story even further. He cannot opt out of the story without abandoning the literary form he has chosen.

This probably explains Matthew's extraordinary story of the guards at the tomb (see text p.24f above). Scholars agree that this can scarcely be a historical account. Why should the Pharisees expect a resurrection when the apostles do not? Why should guards be set only on the second day rather than from the very beginning? And why should they think up such a self-contradictory alibi? It is more reasonable to suppose that the guards appear (they are in Matthew's account alone) in order to keep the story consistent *as story* once Jewish allegations have been made, very much later than the actual event, of Christian fraud.

This introduces a further formative element, that of apologetic and polemic. The Christian battles being fought at the time of the writing of the gospels, several decades after the resurrection, would inevitably affect their composition. Mention has just been made of Jewish calumnies which might have influenced Matthew's resurrection narrative. Mention should also be made of incipient docetic tendencies in the early Church, which so over-spiritualized the Jesus of the gospels that some people were beginning to question the reality of the common humanity he shared with us, before and after resurrection. This may well have influenced the presentation, in Luke and John, of a risen Christ who ate with his disciples, and who could be touched and felt and handled by them.

OLD TESTAMENT HOPES

But why did the evangelists choose to speak of Jesus' resurrection in terms of an empty tomb and the re-vivification of a corpse? Here the influence of the Old Testament, and even more of the literature which bridged the gap between the two Testaments, must be recognized.

The hopes of the Old Testament, at least in its closing phases, had been directed towards the future Day of the Lord and the coming of the Kingdom of God. The many attempts made in the past to achieve the golden age of men's dreams had all ended in failure. Disillusioned, the Old Testament concluded that God's Kingdom was not to be brought about by human means within history. It needed the coming of God himself at the "End" of history. To express these hopes it had used the only language available to men, the language of crisis. The earth-shaking event of God's final intervention could only be expressed in cosmic terms of earthquakes, the disruption of the heavenly bodies, the turning upside down of the order of nature, and the invasion of earth by heaven.

All scholars agree that this kind of Old Testament imagery lies behind Matthew's description of Jesus' death and resurrection in terms of an earthquake, the splitting of the rocks, the advent of darkness and the appearance of an angel (Matthew 27:45 and 51; 28:2). These are not literal descriptions; he has simply used conventional symbolism to indicate that this event marked the decisive intervention of God at the end of history.

But the same is true also of his imagery of tombs opening and the dead being raised. He uses this imagery to describe not only Easter Day but Good Friday itself. Five hundred years earlier Ezekiel had already spoken of his hopes for the survival of exiled Israel in terms of an army of dry bones being covered with flesh and infused with new life (Ezekiel 37). This is clearly nothing more than a bold use of metaphor, applied to the nation as a whole. By the second century BC the book of Daniel had applied the imagery to individuals who had died in the Maccabean struggle and had therefore missed the eagerly awaited coming of God's Kingdom. They would be raised from their graves to partake in the final glory (Daniel 12:2; see 2 Maccabees 7:9ff.). While the Sadducees always refused to take this hope literally, it was strongly championed by Pharisaism, and also by the apocalyptic writers who composed the works which never made their way into the Old Testament — 4 Esdras, the Ethiopian Enoch, and the Syrian Baruch. To express their hopes for the future intervention of God, they all speak in terms of the opening of tombs and the raising of the dead.

When the evangelists adopt this way of speaking, perhaps they mean no more than that, according to their understanding of Jesus' death, the hopes of the apocalyptists had been fulfilled. In this man, the longed-for Kingdom had come; the breakthrough into a new world had been achieved. The old order had ended and the New Age had dawned. To say "the dead were raised from their tombs" means, first and foremost, that the End has come, and that a new phase in man's history (indeed the last) has begun.

STORY AND HISTORY

Dramatization, consistency, apologetic, polemic, apocalyptic imagery — these are some of the elements which went into the making of the Easter stories and allowed the evangelists to turn the Easter event into narrative. Of course the danger is that, having been "historicized" in this way, the stories may then unreflectively be taken for history. James Mackey warns us: "When the mind stops on its journey to God it takes its symbols literally" (op. cit. p. 229). It needs some reflection to realize that

43

the stories do not describe some event — a raising from the dead, an empty tomb, appearances — *upon which* faith was subsequently built. It was the other way round. What came first was the faith-experience, and the stories are a subsequent pictorial elaboration of that experience.

As I have already explained, we cannot touch the fact of resurrection itself, only the faith of the community in its various expressions. But perhaps we can try to put our finger more accurately on what the faith essentially is. If so far we have only handled stories, what is the reality underlying them all? What *really* happened?

CHAPTER THREE

What Really Happened?

"The difficulty is," remarks one scholar, "not whether to believe in the resurrection, but what it is that is to be believed" (C.F. Evans, *Resurrection and the New Testament*, SCM, London 1970, p. 123). In other words, the reality we are looking for is something beyond and other than the stories of the empty tomb and the appearances. These stories are vital as expressions of this reality. In fact, after the complex arguments of theologians, one turns back to the stories with a sigh of relief for their simplicity and charm. But the stories are not indentified with the reality for which we are searching. Where else can we look to find this reality? I would like to suggest a few areas.

THE DEATH OF JESUS

One of the reasons why we have difficulty in understanding the resurrection is that we too easily disassociate it from the death of Jesus. We treat the death and resurrection as if they were two events. In reality they are simply two aspects of the same event, and both aspects challenge us with exactly the same question. As Bonhoeffer said, "Belief in the resurrection is not the solution of the problem of death" (*Letters and Papers from Prison*, Fontana, London 1959, p.93).

This has always been appreciated by those who have thought deeply about death, even those to whom the gospel of Jesus has not been preached. A charming legend of the New Zealand Maoris tells of the attempt made by their folk-hero Maui to overcome death, so that man might live for ever. His father warns him that no man can conquer the death-goddess Hinenuitepo. But Maui is determined to attempt the impossible on behalf of his fellow men, even if he should die in the attempt. He takes into his confidence the birds of the forest — "the tits, robins, saddlebacks, grey warblers, fantails, silver eyes, even the tiny rifleman" — and together with them approaches the fearful icy goddess where she lies asleep. In awe they watch him strip naked, his skin shimmering in the light escaping from beneath Hinenuitepo's eyelids, and then stoop to make his way head first into her body. His struggle through her dark body is long, but eventually he emerges head first through her mouth. His near victory excites the fantails into a burst of delighted laughter. This awakens the goddess, who closes her thighs on him and breaks his body in two. "So ended, in laughter and disgrace, Maui's attempt to conquer death, and, because of his failure, the children of men continue to tread the dark path to Hinenuitepo."

The story bears a striking resemblance to the gospel. In one way it says the very opposite of the resurrection story: Maui did not succeed in overcoming death, Jesus did. But even the Christian has to take seriously the fact that his hero also died in the attempt.

We Christians, with our talk of Jesus' death *and* resurrection, tend to regard this climax of his life as presenting us with two different questions. Until recently we chose his death as the more important of the two, and looked on the resurrection as a kind of optional extra. It was an unexpected bonus which was not strictly neccessary. We could explain the meaning of Jesus' life perfectly well in terms of Calvary alone. It was there that the sacrifice was offered which made satisfaction for men's sins; it was there that the infinite merits were acquired which atoned for the guilt of the world. Our theology was death-oriented. We were crucifixion Christians, and our song was *Miserere*. D.H. Lawrence diagnosed the imbalance long ago and was loud in his complaint:

> The Churches loudly assert: we preach Christ crucified! — But in so doing, they preach only half of the Passion, and do only half their duty. The creed says: "Was crucified, dead, and buried . . . the third day He rose again from the dead." And again "I believe in the resurrection of the body . . . ." So that to preach Christ Crucified is to preach half the truth.
>
> It is the business of the Church to preach Christ born among men — which is Christmas; Christ crucified, which is Good Friday; and Christ Risen, which is Easter. and After Easter, till November and All Saints, and till Annunciation, the year belongs to the Risen Lord: that is all the full-flowering spring, all summer and the autumn of wheat and fruit, all belong to Christ Risen.
>
> But the Churches insist on Christ Crucified and rob us of the blossom and fruit of the year (*The Risen Lord*, in *Phoenix II, Uncollected Works by D.H. Lawrence,* Heinemann, London, 1968, p. 570).

Whether out of deference to Lawrence or not, there has been, in recent years, a shift of interest towards the resurrection. The difficulties we have in understanding the resurrection will never be solved until we see that it is one and the same mystery as the death of Jesus. They are not two events separated from each other by some days. In reality they are the same event. Paul Tillich writes:

> Resurrection is not something added to the death of him who is the Christ; but it is implied in his death. . . . No longer is the universe subjected to the law of death out of birth. It is subjected to a higher law, to the law of life out of death by the death of him who represented eternal life (*The New Being*, SCM Press, London, 1963, p. 178).

47

Ernst Käsemann makes the same point:

> Christ, exalted above the cross in his sublimity, is
> misunderstood if one separates the exaltation from the
> cross, and so reduces their relationship to that of two
> merely consecutive events. The Risen and Exalted One
> remains the Crucified one; and his sovereignty is not
> understood and acknowledged if the cross is merely
> made the last station on his earthly way. . . .
>
> Anyone knowing merely the risen Lord who
> has left his cross behind is no longer speaking of Jesus
> of Nazareth. . . a theology of resurrection that does
> not become a theology of the cross is bound to
> lead . . . to wrong-headed enthusiasm. . . . There is
> no sharing in the glory of the risen Lord except in the
> discipleship of the cross (*Jesus Means Freedom*, SCM
> *Press, London* pp. 67,82,83).

Tillich and Käsemann are propounding novel views of their
own. They are saying no more than what was already said in
John's gospel. John never speaks of Jesus' death without referring to his resurrection, nor of his resurrection without referring to his death. Again and again the cross is spoken of as the
lifting up of Jesus in glory. The Spirit is described as pouring
out of his side in death, and the risen Christ is portrayed as still
able to show his wounds. The author of the book of Revelation
says the same when he brings Jesus' death and resurrection
together in the single image of the lamb that is at once slain and
yet alive. The Eastern Christians say the same when they
celebrate their Good Friday liturgy with flowers and alleluias.
In Jerusalem the very stones of the mother church of Christen-
dom say the same by housing both Calvary and the Sepulchre
under one roof.

We should never speak of the resurrection as if it were
something distinct from Jesus' death. We should never speak of
the resurrection as if it had nothing to do with Jesus' death, so
that Jesus could quite well have died again on the fourth day
and it would not have mattered, because he had proved himself
once and for all on the third day. We should never speak of the
resurrection as if it were simply a prodigious miracle which

reversed the death he had suffered three days earlier, and which Jesus could well have performed three days earlier, only the delay gave it more impact.

Jesus never recovers from his death. The hands and sides he shows to his disciples and to his Father are everlastingly wounded. To believe in the resurrection is to accept Jesus' death as the event in which we find salvation and discover that Jesus lives on. Or, to put it the other way around, to believe that Jesus' death is the world's salvation *is* to believe that he is risen. The resurrection is nothing other than the death of Jesus seen with the eyes of God. "What was from our side death was from the Father's side resurrection" (Gabriel Moran, *Theology of Revelation*, Burns & Oates, London 1967, p. 74). "The doctrine of the incarnation tells the story of Jesus as a tale of the way of the Son of God into the far country, and the doctrine of the resurrection tells the story of Jesus as a tale of the homecoming of the Son of Man. But these two stories are not stories about two consecutive sequences of events. They are the two ways in which we truly narrate one single history, one single sequence of events, the history of Jesus" (Nicholas Lash, *Easter Meaning*, Heythrop Journal XXV (1984), p.12).

In short, Jesus did not die by one agency and rise by another. The very same power which killed him makes him live on. We speak of him as dying the death which comes to all men, or dying because of the sin which he undertook to bear for mankind, or because of the jealousy and narrowness of man. These explanations are all true as far as they go. But they do not go far enough. The true cause of his death was his love, which kept him attached to the cross when he could have avoided it. And it was love he wanted people to believe in, because that is what God is. Yet the same love which killed him also makes him live on in anyone else who echoes that love in his own life. The point is sensitively put in a poem by Clare Richards:

> Christ on the cross,
> Not crushed by death,
> But broken by his love too deep for knowing;
> Christ on the cross,
> Not crushed by death,
> But living on in love too deep for crushing.

Christ on the cross,
Not slain for sin,
But broken by his love too great for giving;
Christ on the cross,
Not crushed by death,
But living on in love too great for slaying.

Christ on the cross,
Not killed by man,
But broken by his love too strong for holding;
Christ on the cross,
Not crushed by death,
But living on in love too strong for killing.

RISING AND RAISING

The difficulties we have in understanding the resurrection will never be solved until we see it in terms of what God did rather than of what Jesus did.

Our English versions of the New Testament have misled us here. They have accustomed us to thinking of the resurrection in terms of a "rising" from the dead, and suggested the image of Jesus reanimating his own corpse. But the word normally used in the original Greek text is not the active verb "to rise"; it is the passive verb "to be raised." [1] The New Testament does not state that Jesus rose, but that he was raised. The resurrection is a statement about God, and about how he is related to the Jesus who died.

It is unfortunate that because of this mistranslation most people have thought of the resurrection as a rising rather

---

[1] The mistranslation is largely due to the influence of the Latin Vulgate. In all fairness, its *surrexit* ("he rose") is not an impossible translation since the Greek verb in question has not only a transitive but also an intransitive sense. But in view of the numerous professions of faith in the New Testament clearly pointing to the Father of our Lord Jesus Christ and the agent of the resurrection, scholars are agreed that the word should everywhere be rendered transitively "he was raised." New versions have taken note. Another Greek verb occasionally used of the resurrection more clearly means "he rose," but it is far less common.

than a raising. The resurrection was put into the category of Jesus' earthly miracles (though it is interesting how often the gospels attribute these also to God), and simply made into a further apologetic proof of his divinity: he rose from the dead by his own independent power. But the New Testament does not think of Jesus' divinity as something which can be proved in such a way, nor of the resurrection as "something extra Jesus had to do" after dying. For the New Testament, the resurrection is an act not of Jesus but of God.

But this too must not be misunderstood. It is not as if God had "to do something extra" to raise Jesus from the dead. The resurrection is a statement about how God stands in relation to such a death as the crucifixion, which in the eyes of the onlookers is the accursed death of an outcast. It is a profession of faith that the God who had apparently abandoned Jesus *in extremis* was in fact even more lovingly present: he loved to such an extent that he trusted his Son utterly, and even allowed him to die. But that death could not break the loving presence of a God who had sworn to be faithful to man for ever. The closeness of God which had been evident throughout Jesus' life was seen in his death to be marvellously beyond anything death can touch. In fact, death had united him more gloriously to God than even his life had been able to portray. He had died more deeply *into* God. God had exalted Jesus into a new kind of life which death can no longer affect. Jesus lives on after death, by the power of God. And it is this power, not Jesus' dexterity, which is proclaimed by those who believe in the resurrection.

TAKING FAITH SERIOUSLY

The difficulties we have in understanding the resurrection will never be solved until we do justice to the word "faith" in this context.

We tend to belittle faith in the resurrection. Faith, we think, is "only" a weak and poor substitute for the "real" experience of seeing the risen Christ. By contrast with the latter it is "mere faith."

Yet seeing the risen Christ and believing in the resurrection are one and the same thing. The first is simply a more concrete way of expressing that faith. Certainly, stories of seeing and hearing and touching Christ *seem* more "real," but that is only because the stories have exteriorized and objectified a spiritual reality. It is no less real when it is expressed in terms of faith. When the disciples grasped the fact that Jesus was not abandoned by God in his death, they "saw" the risen Christ. They did not see him first and only subsequently come to faith.

Faith *is* the meeting with the risen Christ. The believer becomes aware of and "sees" what he has been unable to see before. That is why Paul is able to use the same Greek word *ōphthē* to describe his vision on the Damascus road (when his companions are explicitly stated to have seen *nothing*, Acts 9:7) as he and the evangelists use to describe the Easter day appearances. His "seeing" of Christ is not somehow inferior because it feels less "material" than the experiences of the disciples in the gospel stories. Paul insists:

> Am I not an apostle? Have I not seen Jesus our Lord?
> (1 Corinthians 9:1)
> Paul, an apostle who does not owe his authority to men or his appointment to any human being, but who has been appointed . . . by God the Father who raised Jesus from the dead . . . who called me through his grace and chose to reveal his Son in me (Galatians 1:2 and 15).

Paul met the risen Christ *in* that revelation. That meeting is the real Easter. And the same must be true of anyone's meeting with Jesus. Anyone who truly believes in Jesus knows that even if he dies he still lives on — in fact that he will not lose his life in death at all, because Jesus *is* the resurrection of the body (John 11:25-26). To accept that in faith is to have all the resurrection that there is.

Willi Marxsen illustrates the point by envisaging a person coming to faith and committing himself to the gospel through hearing a sermon. If that person were eventually to ask to whom he actually committed himself in making such a venture of faith, the preacher would have to say: to Jesus. Jesus therefore clearly lives, otherwise the believer could not have been called to faith by him, a faith which he knows to be a reality. Marxsen continues:

> But am I now to try to make the reality of faith doubly sure? Am I even to call in question the possibility of this reality as I have experienced it by making it dependent on some other, allegedly required reality, which is quite irrespective of my faith? That would again mean denial of faith as a venture. The person, therefore, who is shocked when I say that talk of the resurrection of Jesus is an interpretation designed to express the fact that my faith has a source and that source is Jesus — this person can really only be shocked because he is now required *really* to make the venture of faith; he can only be shocked because he suddenly discovers that up to now he had not really ventured at all, that up to now he has not — *believed*!
> (*The Resurrection of Jesus of Nazareth*, SCM Press, London 1970, pp. 142-3).

The closing lines of the fourth gospel provide a perfect illustration of the point being made here. The Doubting Thomas refuses to believe in the risen Christ without first hand evidence. Only when this evidence is finally provided ("Put your finger here; look, here are my hands. Give me your hand; put it into my side") does his disbelief give way to belief. But Jesus' final words are not words of congratulation. On the contrary, Thomas is scolded with the words, "You believe because you can see me. Happy are those who have not seen me and yet believe" (John 20:24-29).

I don't know anyone who actually accepts those words as true. No one I know, given the choice, would opt for "only" believing in the risen Christ, rather than physically seeing him, perhaps even touching him. Seeing, they say, is believing.

The evangelist would say to them, "You are right. What Thomas does in the story obviously feels more real than what people do who do not literally see or touch. But don't you realize that is only because it *is* a story, which deliberately dramatizes the fact that the risen Christ is a reality, not an illusion? Outside the story, that fact can only be grasped by faith."

In other words, the punchline of the story is a plea not to take the story literally. Only those who do take it literally will imagine that Thomas is in a more fortunate position than they are. In the real world, he is not. In the real world, believing that Christ is risen cannot mean physically touching him, whether we are talking of the first disciples of Jesus or the last. The story is the final and most brilliant example of the paradoxical humor which characterises the whole of the fourth gospel.

We minimize faith when we try to avoid the challenge it offers us. Those who ask for tangible and demonstrable proofs over and above what they call their faith are simply showing that they have never arrived at real faith in the resurrection at all. They want "only" to see Christ rather than believe in him. At heart they are really rationalists.

OUR OWN RESURRECTION

The difficulties we have in understanding Jesus' resurrection will never be solved until we learn to re-associate it with our own resurrection.

First of all, the resurrection we picture ourselves enjoying at the end. For pictorial purposes we may imagine a miraculous gathering together of our scattered cells and molecules to form our resurrection-bodies. But this is a picture language. No one who has sung "Ilkley Moor Baht 'At" will be in any doubt about the difficulties involved in literally reconstituting corpses which have passed through worms and ducks and have then gone to build up other bodies!

But in any case, what sort of a "body" would it be that people could dispense with for some years or centuries, and then receive back as a kind of celestial bonus or eternal decoration? Does not the doctrine of the resurrection of the body mean something more worthwhile than that? Does it not have something to say about the state of affairs here and now?

Certainly the New Testament places all the emphasis on the present:

By this we know that we have passed from death to life,
by the love we have for each other (1 John 3:14).

54

The attitude we take towards our fellow human beings is the only indication we shall ever have of whether there is such a thing as resurrection. There is no other resurrection apart from the one which people experience today. Resurrection is not something different from the experience of Christ living on in us, of the Spirit of Jesus manifesting itself in our everyday living. And this need be nothing spectacular. H. A. Williams writes:

> Resurrection as a present miracle . . . is to be found precisely within the ordinary round and daily routine of our lives. Resurrection occurs to us as we are, and its coming is generally quiet and unobtrusive and we may hardly be aware of its creative power. It is often only later that we realize that in some way or other we have been raised to newness of life (*True Resurrection* Mitchell Beazley, London 1972, p. 10).

Every time I know the forgiveness of others, or know that others are forgiven, I know that life has overcome death. Every time I see barriers falling so that the truth can emerge, however painfully, I see life victorious over death. Every time I witness prejudice being broken through, or pity aroused, or hope born in a world which seems to offer so little reason for hope, I am witnessing resurrection. Every time I struggle to understand these things, or show patience over them, or even anger — because after all I could simply wearily dismiss them — I show that I am dealing with something worthwhile, and that too is resurrection.

We are reluctant to admit that such ordinary and even trivial matters can have anything to do with resurrection. We are tempted to think that our lives are too petty and too humdrum to be the scene where God's revelation takes place. Surely, we think, religion is something far more splendid than that! Surely resurrection is a mystery too great to be revealed in the events of my everyday life!

St. Paul shows no such false modesty. Again and again in his letters he puts the resurrection of Christ in the strictest parallelism, not with a speculative resurrection of the future, but with the sort of Christian life he presumes is here and now being led by his readers. A few quotations will make the point:

> When we were baptized we went into the tomb with him (Christ Jesus) and joined him in death, so that as Christ was raised from the dead by the Father's glory, we too might (be raised from the dead, that is to say) *live a new life* (Romans 6:4).

> When through our sins we were (like Christ) dead, God brought us to live with Christ and raised us up with him, and gave us here and now (through the *forgiveness of our sins*) a place with him in heaven (Ephesians 2:5-6).

> You have been buried with him (Christ) when you were baptized; and by baptism, too, you have been raised up with him *through faith* in the God who raises the dead (Colossians 2:12).

> You have been brought back to life with Christ (and this means that) *your thoughts must now* be on heavenly things (Colossians 3:1-2).

It is true that on occasions Paul uses the future tense rather than the present, to indicate that the parallelism of which he is talking is not yet complete. Our new life in Christ always falls short of the ideal:

> If in union with Christ we have imitated his death, we *shall also* imitate him in his resurrection (Romans 6:5).

> He who raised Jesus from the dead *will give* life to your own mortal bodies (Romans 8:11).

> All of us who possess the first-fruits of the Spirit groan inwardly as we *wait for* our bodies to be set free (Romans 8:23).

> The Lord Jesus Christ *will* transfigure these wretched bodies of ours into copies of his glorious body (Philippians 3:21).

But the Christian life spoken of here is never simply in the future. It has already begun, and it is not different from our own future resurrection, or from the past resurrection of Christ in which it is grounded. The transformation we are now undergoing is of the same nature as the transformation which was effected in Jesus at his resurrection. The epistle to the Romans in particular, though it often turns to the future tense to mark the incomplete character of this life, keeps on reverting to the past and the present tense to insist that this life has begun:

> Christ, having been raised from the dead, will never die again . . . so you too must consider yourselves *to be* dead to sin, and (here and now) alive for God (6:9-11).

> You should consider yourselves dead men *brought back* to life (6:13).

> The Spirit of God *has made* his home in you (as he did in the risen Christ) (8:9).

> If Christ *is* in you, then your spirit *is* life itself, because you have been justified (8:10).

> The Spirit bears witness that we *are* (here and now) children of God, and heirs, co-heirs with Christ (who in his resurrection was proclaimed the Son of God) (8:16-17).

> We were specially chosen long ago, and destined to *become* (here and now) images of God's Son (8:29).

> God called those he intended, and justified them, and with them *shared* (here and now) his glory (8:30).

The quotations indicate the extent to which our thinking on Christ's resurrection is incomplete until we link it with our own resurrection, and therefore with our own present living of the Christian life. The resurrection is not a problem to be solved, but an experience to be caught up in. We are not spectators at Christ's resurrection; we are called to be involved.

To concentrate on a resurrection in the past or on a resurrection in the future will very effectively prevent most people from believing in a resurrection here and now. For the eternal life which is promised by the gospel and proclaimed by the church is not a post-mortem life to be lived later on "in eternity." It is life lived in depth at the present moment, so rich with promise that in it eternity has begun. Those who have experienced it know that not even eternity will be able to exhaust it. Muhammad Ali expressed the idea neatly when he recently said : "You don't want no pie in the sky when you die, you want something here on the ground while you're still around." So did D. H. Lawrence: "You thought *consummatum est* meant *all is over*. You were wrong. It means: *The step is taken*. Rise, then, men of the Risen Lord, and push back the stone . . . The Lord is risen as Lord indeed; let us follow, as lords in deed" (*Resurrection*, in *Phoenix, Posthumous Papers of D. H. Lawrence*, Heinemann, London, 1936, p. 739).

When people ask whether we believe in a life after death, we should make it clear that we believe first of all in a life before death. Louis Evely has put it in this way:

> The question should not be, "Do you believe in eternal life?" It should be, "Do you want to live forever, and do you have what it takes?" I am not being flippant. How many people could stand to live forever? There is no worse punishment for someone who does not love; but there is no greater reward for someone who loves. What is important is not the eternalization itself, but that which we have to eternalize. When we see certain assemblies of Christians, we are tempted to pray, "Lord, do not eternalize them now! They are not even breathing." (*The Gospels Without Myth*, New York 1971, pp. 156–7).

This is the area we should be thinking of in speaking of our own resurrection. And if the resurrection of Christ is the very paradigm of our own, why should we expect his to have taken place at a different level of reality?

THE PRESENCE OF CHRIST

The difficulties we have in understanding Jesus' resurrection will never be solved until we have revised our understanding of how Christ is present for us today.

For many people Christ's real presence among his believers seems to mean his real absence. Where he is really present, they think, is somewhere else — in heaven, with God, but not here. All that we have here is the "effect" of his presence elsewhere.

But surely what the resurrection means is that he can never absent himself from his brethren any more. There are now no longer any limits, as there were in the days of his flesh, to the ways in which he is able to be present to his friends. I was recently pulled up sharp by a Christian writer's statement that "Jesus has come and gone." Surely, for someone who believes in the resurrection, Jesus never goes.

Christians speak of the human community as the "Body of Christ." They should take this title seriously. It is not meant to be a metaphor but a sober statement of fact. To say that the body of Jesus was raised or exalted means precisely that he is now *more* embodied than he was before, that he is now able to act upon the world through people instead of through eyes, head, brain, mouth and hands. The body through which he mediated his presence during his earthly life in Palestine has been transformed by death into a new Body, in which he is now *fully* embodied, communicable not just to a few but to millions.

Some people may be shocked at such an analysis of the title "Body of Christ." After all, the risen Body of Christ is something which Christians worship. To call people his Body would mean that it is *they* whom they should adore! Yet what else did Paul mean when he described his conversion as a realization that his persecution of Christians had been a persecution of Jesus himself? What else did the Christian husband mean when, in the older form of the marriage ceremony, he said to his bride, "With my body I thee worship"? What else have Christian saints meant, through the centuries, in kissing the feet of the poor and the sick, in whom above all they recognized the presence of Christ? Where else can Christ be discovered except in the members of his Body? The presence of Christ which Christians celebrate in the liturgy would be a sheer blasphemy if they did not recognize his real presence in each other. St. Teresa of Avila wrote:

> Christ has no body now on earth but yours; no hands
> but yours; no feet but yours; yours are the eyes
> through which is to look out Christ's compassion to
> the world; yours are the feet through which he is to go
> about doing good; yours are the hands with which he
> is to bless men now.

It would seem that artists and poets are quicker to recognize
this truth than others. The Liverpool sculptor Arthur Dooley,
in a BBC interview on the 10 ft. statue of the risen Christ which
he was making for a Methodist church, spoke of it as "a man
diving out of the tomb, winning, with the chains on his wrist
broken; this is liberated man . . . that's what I was trying to get
at — all races freeing themselves from exploitation; for me,
that's Christ." When he was asked whether he in fact believed
in the resurrection he replied:

> I don't know whether it's true or not, but I'd *like* to
> believe it. Christ without the resurrection, he's dead
> anyway! So it's an idea I'd like to buy, (especially)
> when we think of the whole of mankind as being
> Christ. . . . The kind of resurrection I want is when
> all men stand up.
> *Interviewer*: Is this the sort of Christ that you think
> the church stands for now?
> *Arthur Dooley*: No, but it's what it *should* stand
> for. . . . It's a middle-class image of Christ that the
> church pushes. But the real worker Christ, the peo-
> ple's, we're still looking for that. The resurrection is
> missing, that's the first thing. It's the deadness we
> want to do away with. We want the live resurrection.
> And secondly, the image of Christ as all mankind is
> missing too. We want the real man. We want *us*.
> *Interviewer*: Where would you expect to find him if
> he were alive today?
> *Arthur Dooley*: Where I *do* find him. He's on the
> docks. He's the coal man. He's everybody.
> *Interviewer*: "Will the Real Jesus Christ Stand Up?"
> That's the title of this series. What does that mean to
> you?

Arthur Dooley: What it means to me is when we throw
off the chains of exploitation that are holding us down,
and the whole world stands up. And it's not just standing up, we're all going to move. It's not just a passive
thing, we're going to have a go. Revolution and resurrection for me are the same thing.

The language is bold, forthright, "untheological." But then so is
the language of the New Testament, with its uncompromising
statements:

You know, surely, that your bodies are members making up the body of Christ (1 Corinthians 6:15).

You together are Christ's body; each of you is a different part of it (1 Corinthians 12:27).

All of us, in union with Christ, form one body, and as
parts of it we belong to each other (Roman 12:5).

It is men, with their faith, who constitute the Body of Christ.
They *are* the risen Body. There is no other. Take away people,
and Jesus would be a nonentity. He does not exist somewhere
else, separated from or independently of his body. Does anyone?

WHAT REALLY HAPPENED?

To sum up. If the resurrection stories as told in the gospel pages
are not descriptive but symbolic, what did the reality behind
them consist of? What *really* happened?

What happened was that Jesus died a death which, far
from signalling his end, really marks the beginning of his story.

What happened was that God was revealed in that death
as a God who did not abandon Jesus, but exalted him to a new
life.

What happened was that the disciples committed themselves to a living Christ, not to the memory of a dead one.

What happened was that this experience of the disciples
marked the beginning of a way of life in which they recognized
that eternity had begun.

What happened was that from then on the living Christ
has never ceased to be present wherever men live as he lived and
died.

CHAPTER FOUR

Explaining the Resurrection Away?

The explanation of the resurrection given in these pages will disturb some people. They may want to refer back to the Pauline statement quoted in the foreword, that "if Christ has not been raised, then our preaching is useless and your believing it is useless" (1 Corinthians 15:14), with the implication that the analysis so far given has in effect explained the resurrection away.

It has not been my intention to explain anything away. To demythologize the resurrection does not mean to get rid of it, only to put a more accurate finger on where the reality of it lies. All Christians, whether they are conservatives or liberals, profess their faith in the risen Christ. The problem remains, what does this mean? The questions I have posed — and they are no more than an echo of the questions posed by today's scholars — are not designed to make the resurrection less real; quite the contrary. Far from blunting that reality for the reader, it is my hope that they will sharpen it.

MISGIVINGS

All the same, many people will complain that this explanation has made the resurrection *feel* a lot less than it used to. Beforehand, with Jesus actually eating fish and Thomas physically putting his hand into Christ's side, it seemed so objective that it was tangible. Now it seems to have been reduced to something dangerously subjective. They may grant the force of the scholar's arguments about the empty tomb and acknowledge that this is not strictly needed for an understanding of the resurrection. They may admit the inadequacy of the concept of reanimating a corpse, and agree not to insist on this as an essential part of the resurrection. They may even concede that the visible appearances of the risen Christ to the disciples as reported in the gospel stories need not have been as visible as all that. But if what the scholars say means that the disciples did not even have some shattering objective experience, some rock-solid demonstrable proof, only some sort of "realization," then they will want to know the difference between that and no resurrection at all!

Beforehand, a *real* resurrection gave rise to the faith of the apostles. Now the faith of the apostles seems to give rise to a merely *imaginary* resurrection. The scholars seem to have watered the resurrection down to such an extent that the ordinary Christian can no longer see what is left. In what sense is the resurrection any longer part of the history of mankind?

THE RESURRECTION UNHISTORICAL

I recently spent a very instructive morning in the galleries of the Venice *Accademia*. Housing as it does an extraordinarily rich collection of paintings of every century, this museum offers to the visitor a better opportunity than most of studying the development of western art.

I was particularly interested in the Renaissance galleries and the evidence they provide of the bold and irreversible step taken in the fourteenth century. Before then all the paintings were couched in the Byzantine mode. Everything was formalized according to the strictest canons, every detail stylized, and the symbolism of each theme so universally agreed that it was possible to learn the language of that symbolism simply by walking from one painting to another.

The discovery of perspective by the Renaissance artists was a brilliant breakthrough. But it also introduced into religious art a confusion which had never existed before. All the traditional symbols continued to be used, but since they were now expressed in naturalistic terms they began to demand a literal interpretation. A naturalistic Christ stepping out of a naturalistic tomb into a naturalistic garden — what else could this be but a still from a film? None of the pre-Renaissance paintings of the ascension can be interpreted as anything other than a symbol of Christ's "ascendancy." None of the post-Renaissance ones can be interpreted as anything other than the historical portrayal of a space-flight. The symbol had been turned into a photograph and was no longer recognizable as symbol.

A similar confusion has bedeviled the understanding of the gospels from the earliest times. When the evangelists made their bold decision to express their faith in narrative form rather than in abstract discourse, they ran the risk of being interpreted historically. "On Monday morning Jesus went to such and such a place and cured so and so, and then in the afternoon delivered the following discourse; on Tuesday he travelled so many miles to another town, where the following dispute took place, etc."

For the narratives that have to do with the events of Jesus' earthly life, this biographical reading does little harm except to keep the reader at a fairly superficial level and prevent him from appreciating the profound theology contained in the narrative. But when this historicization is extended into the resurrection stories the results are disastrous. The risen Christ becomes simply a reanimated corpse, a being of earth who, after an unfortunate interruption of three days and before finally disappearing forever, walks and talks with his friends in exactly the way he did before. His post-mortem biography is as tangible and demonstrable as was his conduct before he died.

Yet the gospel was never intended to be a biography of this kind, least of all the pages devoted explicitly to the resurrection. These do not simply keep a videotaped record of something that happened in the past; they proclaim a fact which is of permanent significance because it transcends time and space. The gospel was written to bring its readers face to face with a Christ who is their contemporary because he lives on into the present. Here too the symbol, able to bring about such an encounter, must not be taken for a photograph which cannot. The gospel is not a mere chronicle of past events; it is a profession of faith challenging the reader now to a decision about the Christ presented to him.

It may be objected: all the same, this profession of faith must be based on something historical. However symbolic the resurrection stories may be, they would be nothing more than stories if they were not rooted in something that actually happened.

This is true. The question remains whether "history" is the right word for this. History is concerned with what can be assessed, demonstrated and verified. It deals with events which take place in time and space. It is concerned with who did what to whom, where and when and why.

The resurrection is not an event of that kind. It is an event of the same order as the glorification of Christ, his ascension into heaven, and sitting at the right hand of the Father. These are not simply appendices to Calvary, adducible in evidence just as that event was. The resurrection is strictly an "act of God," witnessed by no one, and therefore not the object of a historian's knowledge or subject to his scrutiny. The act by which God raised Jesus is unique and outside the laws by which a historian works. The historian can know of its effects on people and investigate these, but the act itself lies outside his province because it is, in a sense, the *end* of history, the eschatological event which goes beyond the limits imposed by time and space. Scholars today agree with Thomas Aquinas who said that the resurrection "cannot be demonstrated" (*Summa Theologiae* 3, 55, 5) and therefore is not "historical."

TRANSHISTORICAL

The word "unhistorical" will make many people conclude that, when all the shouting is over, the fact is that *nothing* happened. Their conclusion would be understandable, but wrong. What happened was *not* nothing. What we are dealing with is not something merely imaginary or fictitious. We are dealing with something which is real in the most profound sense of the word. So real in fact that it bursts through the bounds of history, and transcends it.

The word used by theologians to describe such a reality is "transhistorical." The word is meant to indicate that this reality has one foot in "another world." Clearly, an event which is in effect a journey from death into the all-embracing dimension of God can no longer be expressed in terms of history. It goes beyond those terms and can only be described as transcendental. "To be raised from the dead" is an entirely new way of being present to the rest of reality: it is to begin to be with man in the way that God himself is with man. Such an event cannot be regarded simply as a matter of past history. It is an event which transcends history. St. Paul finds he can only express the newness of the situation by speaking of the transformation of the perishable into the imperishable, of that which is held in contempt into that which shares God's own glory, and of that which is weak into that which shares God's own power (1 Corinthians 15:42–43).

Because of the resurrection, Christ belongs to the present, and to all times. We can know about his death by receiving information about it from the past. We can know about his resurrection only by meeting him in the present. Everyone was deeply shocked when Bultmann first coined the phrase, "Christ is risen and ascended into the kerygma." But it contains a profound truth, that the otherwise "transhistorical" event of the resurrection and ascension cannot enter into history except through the preaching of Jesus' disciples and the witness of their lives. If the resurrection is an entry into the fullness of life, no mere physical description of it will ever be able to convince people of its reality: it must be actually experienced.

FAITH AGAIN

So we come back again to the subject of faith. I referred earlier to the fear of some people that the scholars may have reduced the resurrection to something created by the faith of the first witnesses. The fear is unfounded. No scholar suggests that the resurrection is not a reality but only a figment. All the same it remains true that the resurrection can only be recognized or grasped or spoken of in terms of faith. "Without the Christian experience of faith, we have no organ which can give us a view of Jesus' resurrection" (E. Schillebeeckx, *Interim Report on the Books Jesus and Christ*, SCM, London 1980, p. 79). Without this "faith-perspective" the resurrection is simply an unrecognizable event. And obviously an unbeliever, who does not have this perspective, cannot be accused of wilful blindness. He simply cannot "see" what the believer "sees."

This applies, of course, to the first witnesses of the resurrection too. Even they needed faith to appreciate the fact that Jesus had been raised from the dead. We would sometimes like to imagine that they, at least, had solid proof, demonstrable evidence. After all, their witness is foundational, the basis on which the faith of all future generations must rest. If that witness is itself supported on nothing more substantial than their *own* faith, what is to prevent the whole structure from collapsing like a house of cards?

Clearly, people who think like this do not see faith as a very firm foundation! Yet without it the apostles themselves could not have "seen" the risen Christ. No "objective" proof could provide that vision for them, only faith. They could not be spared the scandal of the cross, any more than any other follower of Christ can be.

Any other alternative would be totally unacceptable, as a moment's reflection will show. Marxsen highlights the apostles' resurrection-faith by comparing it with the faith they required to recognize who Jesus was during his ministry:

> It was impossible to tell by looking at him who the earthly Jesus was. They could only believe that he represented God in this world; and they could only believe that when they acceded to his demand. This commitment to what Jesus demanded had no guarantee behind it. Jesus rejected the demand for signs as a preliminary legitimation. He wanted a daring faith.

A verifiable resurrection, with its multiplicity of proofs, would have altered everything in one respect. Jesus would now have received his legitimation. Who he was would now be a matter of certainty. The demand for signs would, so to speak, have been fulfilled. It would have continued to be hard enough for these witnesses to *live* the later life of faith. But it would no longer have been a venture for the witnesses to *enter* on that life. Indeed it would have been a counsel of wisdom; it would now have been simply stupid not to do what Jesus had demanded. The path of the witnesses would no longer have been the path of faith because Jesus' demand would now be law. The witnesses would have been the only people who no longer needed to make the venture of faith and who therefore did not need to believe at all (*op. cit.*, p. 150).

If that conclusion is unacceptable, then it is obvious that the apostles who saw the risen Jesus 2000 years ago are in exactly the same position as I am today. I speak of myself as sharing their faith because I, like them, have to face the real challenge of Jesus, and to answer the question: "Does this crucified one call me to faith? Does he enable me to die and live again?" Our faith is founded not on an empty tomb or on visions, not even on people telling me about them. My faith, like that of the apostles, is founded on Jesus himself, whom I know to be alive because he makes it possible for me today to pass from death to life. I cannot escape this venture of faith. Nor do I find such an explanation of the resurrection more diluted than the classical one.

Marxsen concludes his study of the resurrection by considering what contribution critical research is able to make towards reinstating faith for people who think of "proof" as being very solid and "faith" as being rather shaky:

> Modern theology is sometimes reproached with having ceased to make any demands on people. We are told that it seeks to dispense with the stumbling block of faith and that it takes its bearings from modern man. But this is far from being the case. No theology can make faith any easier. Every individual has to make the venture of faith for himself and no theology

can help him. But theology can make the approach to the real questions of faith easier. For who will deny that there are a great many people who, when they hear anything about the Christian faith, immediately think (after the virgin birth) of the resurrection of Jesus, which they can neither cope with nor see beyond? Hence, Jesus' invitation to believe never reaches them at all. Again, there are other people who commit themselves to Jesus' offer, but who continue to feel scruples about whether they can properly call themselves Christians because, although they make the venture of love, they cannot come to terms with the resurrection (in the [literal] sense in which they conceive it).

If, then, historical-critical research helps to determine the place of the assertion of Jesus' resurrection in the framework of the Christian creed, then it shows by this means that faith in the resurrection of Jesus is not a barrier which has to be overcome first — or even at a later stage. In my view, it is the man who fights for the preservation of this barrier today who is standing in the way of the Christian faith (*op. cit.*, p. 153).

More Than One Way

There is more than one way, Marxsen is saying, of speaking about the resurrection. We have tended to restrict ourselves to one way, and used the language of "rising" or "raising" in which (as we saw above) Jewish apocalyptic writings expressed their hopes about Kingdom Come. The word "resurrection," if pressed, can itself be misleading. It means literally a rising or raising of this kind.

For anyone restricted to this way of thinking, any other expression of the mystery we are considering, such as "appearing to his disciples" or "going to heaven" or "sending down the Spirit" can only be thought of as subsequent to the resurrection. "On the third day he rose again," we proclaim in the creed, and then go on to state, "he ascended into heaven" and later "we believe in the Holy Spirit who proceeds from the Father and the Son," as if these were three distinct phases in a biographical sequence.

St. John, as I pointed out earlier, does not think in terms of such a sequence. For him the crucifixion is already a lifting up (John 3:13) whereby the Son of Man ascends into heaven (6:62), and Jesus can therefore say, "I am ascending to my Father" on Easter day itself (20:17). Similarly, the Water of the Spirit is said to pour from him (19:34), or the Wind of the Spirit to be breathed out of him whether he is considered as dying (19:30) or as rising (20:22). Conversely, the wounds by which he died are not neutralized by the resurrection: they are still so much part of the Easter Christ that the disciple can put his hand in them (20:27). Jesus' death, resurrection, appearance, ascension and sending of the Holy Spirit are not episodes in a biography. They are alternative ways of expressing the same one mystery.

NO RAISING

In the light of this, it should cause no surprise to discover that some New Testament writings never find it necessary to use the imagery of "raising from the dead" at all. Presumably they proclaim the same "risen" Christ who is the subject of all other New Testament writings. They would scarcely be Christian writings unless they did so. Yet 2 Thessalonians, Titus, Philemon, James, 2 Peter, 1, 2 and 3 John, and Jude (and they comprise one sixth of the New Testament epistles) make no reference whatever to the "raising" which we tend to regard as such an essential part of the resurrection. They find it possible to speak of Easter without this language.

So, of course, do many other texts even in writings which otherwise turn readily enough to the imagery of "raising." Peter expresses the mystery at one point in his epistle by pointing to the obverse and the reverse of the event:

70

> He was put to death in the flesh,
> but brought to life in the Spirit (1 Peter 3:18).

A poem in 1 Timothy expresses the contrast in similar words:

> He was made visible in the flesh,
> vindicated in the Spirit (1 Timothy 3:16).

The epistle to the Hebrews, using the imagery of the annual entry of the high priest into the Holy of Holies to make atonement with the blood of animals, speaks of the very death of Jesus (not something which happened subsequently) as constituting his entry into the heavenly sanctuary:

> Christ, who offered himself as the perfect sacrifice to God through the eternal Spirit . . . has entered the sanctuary once and for all, taking with him . . . his own blood (Hebrews 9:11–14).

> By his death he took away all the power of the devil, who had power over death, and set free all those who had been held in slavery all their lives by the fear of death (2:14–15).

NO APPEARANCES

The gospel of Mark, the earliest of the four we now possess, finds it possible to present the heart of the matter without even narrating any appearances of the risen Christ. The gospel ends at 16:8, with the women's discovery of the empty tomb, their realization that the crucified one is not there, and their terrified silence. It is true that the gospel as it now exists contains twelve further verses, 16:9–20, which provide a more detailed ending. But all scholars agree (see p. 19 above) that these verses are not part of Mark's original work. It is possible that his own longer ending has been lost, but scholars more and more tend to the view that Mark intended his gospel to end, dramatically, in silence and awe, at 16:8. He presumably thought that this was the best way of conveying what Easter means. The reader is left to "see" the living Christ for himself.

EXALTATION LANGUAGE

There are texts of the New Testament which use the imagery of "raising up to heaven" as an alternative way of expressing what other texts express in terms of "raising from the dead." It is "up-down" language instead of "before-after" language. One is not an appendix to the other. Exaltation is not meant to add anything to raising from the dead. It is simply another way of speaking of the heavenly significance of what happened to Jesus at Easter. He was glorified and transformed. He was elevated to a level where he shares in God's own power and lordship. He entered into a new, heavenly and godly manner of existence.

Texts like the following, therefore, are not to be taken as poor relations of "resurrection texts." They are exactly equivalent:

> All authority *in heaven* and on earth has (now) been given to me (Matthew 28:18).

> God has made this Jesus whom you crucified *into Lord* (Acts 2:36).

> Jesus Christ our Lord was proclaimed Son of God *in all his power* through his resurrection (Romans 1:4).

> If your lips confess that Jesus is *Lord* (which is another way of saying, If you believe in your heart that God raised him from the dead), you will be saved (Romans 10:9).

> Christ is the one who *rose higher* than all the heavens to fill all things (Ephesians 4:10).

> God raised him *high*, and gave him the Name which is above all other names, so that . . . every tongue should acclaim Jesus Christ as *Lord* (Philippians 2:9–11).

> He was made visible in the flesh . . . and taken up *in glory* (Timothy 3:16).

72

Now that he has destroyed the defilement of sin, he has gone to take his *place in heaven* at the right hand of divine majesty (Hebrews 1:3).

We see in Jesus one who was for a short while made lower than the angels and is now *crowned with glory and splendour* because he submitted to death (Hebrews 2:9).

HE IS ALIVE

Nor does this exhaust the ingenuity of the New Testament in finding ways to speak of the Easter mystery. Some texts resort to the simplest alternative and say, He is alive:

Why look among the dead for someone *who is alive?* (Luke 24:5).

They had seen a vision of angels who declared *he was alive* (Luke 24:23).

He *showed himself alive* to them after his Passion (Acts 1:3).

A dead man called Jesus whom Paul alleged *to be alive* (Acts 25:19).

He was crucified through weakness, and still *he lives now* through the power of God (2 Corinthians 13:4).

In other texts this easily turns into psychological language. That Jesus is alive means above all that he is alive for me and in me. Hence texts like the following are also resurrection texts:

We carry with us in our body the death of Jesus, so that the life of Jesus, too, may be seen *in our body* (2 Corinthians 4:10).

God chose to reveal his Son *in me* (Galatians 1:16).

I live now not with my own life but with the life of Christ who lives *in me* (Galatians 2:20).

I shall have the courage for Christ to be glorified *in my body* (Philippians 1:20).

73

Life *to me*, of course, is Christ (1:21).

The supreme advantage of *knowing* Christ Jesus my Lord (3:8).

I was *grasped* by Christ Jesus (3:12).

It is arguable that the Emmaus story of Luke 24 is a piece of "psychological" writing of this kind. Where in other stories the risen Christ is "seen" and "touched," here his relationship to his disciples is expressed in terms of hearing and eating. It is in the unfolding of the scriptures that the disciples' hearts burn as they hear the risen Christ speaking to them, and in the breaking of bread that they recognize his presence in their midst.

Some people may feel that in speaking of the resurrection in these terms we have reached too "subjective" a level. They need to be reminded once again that none of these expressions of the resurrection must be mistaken for a literal description. Each struggles with language to express the mystery of Jesus' communion with God and how this affects the rest of mankind. All language is relative when it tries to cope with a mystery as deep as this. We can only be grateful that scripture has attempted to convey it in so many diverse ways, and we should resist the temptation to reduce them all to one.

> It is, in principle, possible to make true statements about that to which the language of resurrection refers, without using the terminology, or imagery, of "rising" from the dead. . . . There is a crucial difference . . . between telling a story differently and telling a different story. . . . To refrain from speaking of "rising" is not necessarily to tell a different story (Nicholas Lash, *op. cit.*, p. 16f).

MORE WAYS

In fact, given the variety of these New Testament expressions, we ought to be bold in attempting many more ways of saying what the resurrection means for us today. We shall not pretend, any more than the New Testament did, that any of these can be exclusive or absolute.

To believe in the risen Christ is to believe in the person of Jesus of Nazareth whose whole life proclaimed a God of love and mercy. To believe in the risen Christ is to believe that this reality was not extinguished at death, and that Jesus' love and forgiveness were stronger than the forces which killed him. To believe in the risen Christ is to know that he who was foolish and weak became the wisdom and power of God. To believe in the risen Christ is to believe that on the cross God endorsed Jesus as the person he had shown himself to be throughout his life.

But that still leaves the resurrection too much in the past tense. Let's bring it more closely into the present. To believe in the resurrection means that, for me, Jesus is not a mere memory; he continues to live by the power of God, and to speak to me in my own experience across the frontiers of death. To believe in the resurrection means that I have committed myself to the God revealed to me in Jesus' death, and that he has shown me the face of the living Christ. To believe in the resurrection means that I acknowledge the crucified Jesus as governing the manner of my life. To believe in the resurrection means that I have seen the fulfilment of God's plan for mankind, and that I know myself called to the fullness of life which Jesus has entered.

The resurrection means that Jesus is the resurrection of the body. The resurrection means that Jesus lives on with such a fullness of life that he is able to animate a community of men. The resurrection means that I have seen Jesus return to life and appear in the least of his brethren. The resurrection means that in Jesus, and especially in his death, I have understood something startlingly new about the purpose of my life. The resurrection means that Jesus constantly comes into my life.

To say that the dead was raised to life, that he appeared to his disciples, that he was present at the breaking of bread, and that he sent out his disciples to call others to faith — means that the crucified one is experienced as living in many ways: in the call to faith, at the eucharist, and in the missionary awareness of Christians.

"But these statements," someone will say, "are quite inadequate as expressions of what the resurrection really is."

Of course they are. So is every other statement, including those made by the New Testament authors.

> God has never spoken to anyone other than the way in which he speaks to you. God has never healed anyone other than the way in which he heals you. God has never raised anyone from the dead other than the way in which he raises you from the dead. . . . The gospel narratives and the teachings of the Church . . . do nothing more than express the understanding of the experiences lived by those men who wrote the gospels and formulated the teachings of the Church — an understanding that they now seek to impart to us so that we, too, may grasp the meaning of what we experience in common with them (Louis Evely, *op. cit.*, pp. 68–9).

> The resurrection of Christ occurred so that you and I would have the joy of feeding him, clothing him, giving him blood, making him feel wanted. . . . That Jesus, that hungry Jesus asking for a lump of bread, that naked Jesus asking for clothes, that homeless Jesus needing a house — that Jesus is around the world in every place, looking up at you and me and asking, "Did you love me?" (Mother Teresa of Calcutta)

is it possible
for a man to speak
to another man's heart?
for a man on
a cross
20000 years
upon a hill
to speak
today to
a man's own
heart?
is it possible
for one man's

76

death
to be another
man's life
when that man's
death
2000 years
upon a hill
said death
to his friends
and desolation
to his mother?
is it possible
for one man's
shadow to
throw light
on life and love
2000 years?

is it?
(National Pastoral Institute, Melbourne, 1974)

The Resurrection of the Body

A Feiffer cartoon represents a bodiless head. It is accompanied by a series of statements: "This is my head"; "It thinks, it talks, it charms"; "It worries, it laughs, it hurts"; "It has a hundred wonderful tricks"; "I am proud of it." The statements continue alongside a headless body: "This is my body"; "It is funny-looking, it malfunctions"; "It looks best in winter clothes"; "I have as little to do with it as is humanly possible"; "Lucky for my body that I need it to chauffeur my head around." In the final frame the head returns to say: "Otherwise out it would go."

The cartoon illustrates an attitude with which everyone is familiar. What is important about man is his intellect, his mind, his spirit. The rest is unimportant, in fact an embarrassing encumbrance, which we tolerate because the mind is unfortunately unable to function on its own. For the moment. But it will!

BODY AND SOUL

The attitude which the cartoonist is lampooning stands in stark contrast to the Christian's professed faith in a resurrection of the body. The Christian hope is heir to the Old Testament which, in yearning for man's union with God, naturally included the body in that devoutly wished-for consummation. I have touched on this topic briefly above. I want in this chapter to explore the subject a little more.

The Old Testament never makes the dichotomy which we make so easily today between body and soul, as if these were two separate and separable components of man. Man was thought of as a unity and the whole of him stood in need of salvation, not only the "spiritual" part of him. If man was to be transformed by his union with God, then the body itself had to be transformed. Because man is not saved when his soul has gone to heaven: the body also yearns for God.

But even that does not fully express the truth of the matter. Strictly speaking man's body is not an "also." Man is not split into two in that way. He is not a soul which has unfortunately been embodied. He is a body which has been wondrously animated. He does not merely *have* a body: he *is* a body. And the whole of him longs for God. In short, for biblical man, the word "body" does not mean something that displaces a certain amount of water in the bath. It means what people mean when they say "somebody" or "anybody."

It was the philosophy of Greece which divided man into two, and so depicted salvation as an escape from the body. The soul was destined for immortality, the body for the dustheap. The Hebrews were never able to cope with such an antithesis. They simply could not imagine a disembodied soul. To disembody a man would not be to liberate him but to destroy him. Unless man survived death *as a body* he could not be said to live at all.

It is this way of thinking that Judaism bequeathed to Christianity. The Christian believes — at least he professes to believe — in a resurrection of the body, that is to say, not in the immortality of the soul but in an immortality which is corporeal, in the passing of the total and undivided person into a new mode of existence. So much needs to be said to reinstate the body.

BODY AND FLESH

But this must not be understood in a gross or materialistic way. Most people imagine that having said "resurrection of the body" they have committed themselves to a "resurrection of the flesh." Indeed the Greek and Latin form of the Apostles' Creed, with its *sarkos anastasin* and *carnis resurrectionem* would corroborate such a belief. The crude translation lies behind the centuries-old Christian prohibition of cremation.

But according to biblical thought, "flesh" is precisely what cannot be raised from the dead:

> All flesh is grass which must wither (Isaiah 40:7).

> The flesh is weak (Matthew 26:41).

> To set the mind on the flesh is death (Romans 8:6).

> Those who are in the flesh cannot please God (Romans 8:8).

> If you live according to the flesh you will die (Romans 8:13).

> Flesh and blood cannot inherit the kingdom of God (1 Corinthians 15:50).

> He who sows in the field of his flesh will get a harvest of corruption out of it (Galatians 6:8).

Shakespeare understood this well. He wrote at a time when biblical usage was still current, and he refers quite naturally to

> The heartache and the thousand natural shocks
> That flesh is heir to (*Hamlet* 3,1)

and has his hero yearning

> O, that this too too solid flesh would melt (1,2).

80

While anyone may share those sentiments of Hamlet and feel that the flesh is too much with us, he may not (at least biblically speaking) conclude that the body is. What exactly is the body?

The question is worth asking, not only because in common parlance body is equated with flesh, but because a lot of Christian writers who should know better make the same equation. They stress that Christians believe in a *bodily* resurrection, as if to imply that those who put a question mark over a *fleshly* resurrection (or physical, or tangible, or visible, which is the same thing) are denying the Christian faith. But if the body is not the same thing as the flesh, what exactly is it?

For the Greeks, the body was thought of as the principle of individuation. It is that which marks out the perimeter of a man, and therefore limits him, isolates him and separates him from others. A is A and not B, and B is B and not A, because they inhabit different bodies. The Greek play on words sums up the attitude: *sōma sēma*, the body is a tomb.

For the Hebrews, the body was almost the exact opposite. It was thought of as the principle of communion. It is that by which a man is related to all other men, and indeed to the rest of creation. The body is not a barrier separating people from each other; it is the bridge by which they discover each other, and so relate and communicate with each other. The body means fellowship and brotherhood. The body is not only that by which a man sees others; it is that by which he is seen by others, and therefore the vital link which unites him with all that exists. To be a body means to be kin with all other embodied things, to be part and parcel of the world and history and mankind.

There can be no doubt that this Hebrew way of thinking finds a closer echo in modern man's understanding of himself than the Greek. Our very approach to medicine, psychology and psychiatry depends precisely on an appreciation of man as body, not as an imprisoned soul. We see the body as the very model of the world we live in, and know that as a man is in his body, so will he be in the world. We should respect this model, for it has much to teach us when we are tempted to revert to a Greek intellectualism. The nausea which spontaneously arises

81

in us at the sight of brutality, the sheer bodily outrage and rebellion that we feel, comes from a deeper sense of the holy than the analytic mind will ever be capable of expressing.

Of course, when we have said that the body means relationship and communication with others, it does not follow that this relationship is necessarily strong, or the communication good. In fact, what we usually experience is the very opposite. And we put the blame on this lumpish body of ours, thinking that what we need is a "soul-to-soul" union with others. But what we really need is the transformation of the body, not its elimination. In longing for better communication we are longing for more embodiment, not less. What irks us about our relationship and communion is that it is so crippled, so fractionally operative compared with what it could be. What we are deeply pining for is to be a hundred per cent bodily, that is to say, human. This is precisely what resurrection is about.

BODY AND SPIRIT

The Bible, then, does not distinguish between body and soul. The distinction it makes is between flesh and spirit. Flesh, as we have seen, refers to man's weakness and vulnerability, his perishability and powerlessness. "Man in the flesh" describes above all man in his otherness from the God who is the source of his life, man left to his own resources, man drawn down by his own gravity towards death.

The antithesis of flesh is spirit. In our western languages, the word "spirit" suggests that which is least real in our experience, the nearest thing we know to nothing; the fact that our synonym for spirit is "ghost" speaks volumes. The Hebrew usage is almost the exact opposite of this. Spirit is that which is most real, most full of vitality, activity, creativity and life. "Spirit" in fact is the word that is used to describe the very power and dynamism of God.

Now flesh and spirit are not related in the same way that body and soul are. Body and soul were thought of as two components of man. Flesh and spirit are not. They both describe the whole man. Man remains an undivided totality. And he can be either spirit or flesh, that is to say, animated by God and powerful, or separated from God and weak.

So can the body. In our language, a "spiritual body" sounds like a paradox. The spirit, we think, is the opposite of matter. This is not so in biblical thought, where the word "spiritual" does not mean immaterial or disincarnate. The body *can* be spiritual. Our difficulty is that the body we have experienced is by and large the "body of flesh." We take it for granted that we know what the term "body" means. We do not. Most of our experience is of the "unspiritual body," that is to say, of

> knowing each other only by sight, smell, touch, sympathy, words and intuition; not understanding even ourselves properly; being afraid of people, and things, and even life; feeling oppressed by the sheer size of what is not known; feeling shackled by hatred, prejudice, etiquette, laws and customs; being subject to all the emotions which arise from the monstrous incompleteness of human bodiliness (Rosemary Haughton in *New Christian*, 30 October 1969).

Faith in the resurrection is faith in the possibility of the body breaking through these limitations and becoming totally spiritual, a hundred per cent spirit-filled.

A body of flesh is the prisoner of its environment; a spiritual body is one which has been liberated from this solitary confinement. A body of flesh is something I feel that I own, like a dangerous caged animal, ever preventing me from becoming my true self; a spiritual body is one which I have accepted that I *am*, and which finally allows me to achieve my human potential. We are tempted to think that the one can be slowly improved into the other. The New Testament states that a total transformation is needed, and that this cannot be effected without a death and resurrection. Perhaps many of them.

THE RESURRECTION OF JESUS' BODY

When we speak of Jesus' bodily resurrection, we are speaking of what happened to the whole person of Jesus, not simply to his corpse. We are speaking above all of his communicability to his brethren, because that is what bodiliness is all about.

In the "days of his flesh," his relationship with others was as limited as we experience our own to be. To say that his body has been "raised" means that he died *out* of that body of flesh and became a body of spirit. To put it into the New Testament language, the spirit which had animated Jesus throughout his life, the godly spirit of love which he yearned to share with his disciples, broke through its physical limitations and became available to men in a way which was impossible before.

At first sight such a statement seems to suggest that resurrection means disembodiment. The opposite is true. Through his death Jesus has become more embodied than before. His death does not mean that his communicability has come to an end; it has deepened because his relationship with other men has been restructured. Instead of being, as each of us is, simply an individual numerically distinct from others, he has become one with all men. His "risen body" is not simply an extension of his earthly body; it has entered into a new mode of being which can only be described as an embodied sharing of himself with others. If anyone was asked two thousand years ago where the body of Jesus was, he could only point to the person who walked the lanes of Galilee, and who could be specified in terms of sight, touch, hearing, weight and so on. If anyone is asked today where the body of Jesus is, he can only point to a group of people. They *are* the way in which he is now embodied.

The realization that this was so, that to persecute men was to persecute the Jesus who was embodied in them, transformed the life of Paul. John the evangelist was also acutely aware of this new way in which Jesus was bodily present after his death. In what is known as the Farewell Discourse (John 14–17) he speaks of Jesus' death as an essential part of his glorification. It is both his departure and his return in order to be more deeply present to his disciples. They cannot at present share his physical death. But they can anticipate it in that death to self which is entailed in loving each other. And that love is the coming of the Spirit of Christ; that love is the very presence of Christ; that love is the disciple's own entry into glory. The purpose of his death therefore, Jesus tells his disciples, is

> so that where I am (in heaven, with the Father) you
> may be too (John 14:3).

> Father, I want those you have given me
> to be with me where I am (17:24).

But this can be put into "this-world" language too:

> I will not leave you orphans;
> I will come back to you . . .
> and you will understand that I am in my Father
> and you in me and I in you (14: 18–20).

> Make your home in me, as I make mine in you (15:4).

> Father, I have given them the glory you gave to me,
> that they may be one as we are one.
> With me in them and you in me
> may they be so completely one
> that the world will realize . . .
> that I have loved them as much as you loved me
> (17:22–23).

> I have made your name known to them . . .
> so that the love with which you loved me may be in
> them,
> and so that I may be in them (17:26).

THE RESURRECTION OF OUR BODY

The Christian's own hope of resurrection is his conviction that what has happened to Jesus will happen to him too, and has in fact already begun to happen.

This conviction is not based on some purported vision of the future state of mankind, less still on any report brought back to us from beyond the grave. Quite simply it is based on what the Christian has already experienced here and now. Paul expresses this well when he affirms his certainty that nothing existing in the present or in the future, no power from above or from below, no angel of heaven or king of earth, not even *death* itself, will ever be able to separate him from the love of God which he has discovered in Jesus (Romans 8:38–39). In other words, his present experience of God's love is such that he knows that even death will not be able to destroy it. So that if someone had asked him, "Where will you be when you die?" he could only have answered, "I don't know, but I am certain that I shall continue to be embraced by God's love." And his certainty was rooted in that love as it had been revealed to him in the life and death of Jesus.

The psalmist, even without the example of Jesus before his eyes, had already expressed something of the same conviction when he said again on the basis of his present experience of God's love:

> My heart rejoices, my soul is glad,
> even my body shall rest in safety.
> For you will not leave my soul among the dead
> nor let your loved one see corruption (Psalm 16:9–10).

Safety, or salvation, must include the body. The biblical claim, not only for Jesus but for everyone, is of a bodily salvation. What Paul himself is hoping for in speaking of "me" is a survival not merely of the mind or soul but of the total person, and in his thought-pattern this could not exclude the body.

But again this must not be understood in a materialistic or "fleshly" way. Paul and the psalmist are not predicting some magical reanimation of muscles, organs and arteries. The word "body," as we have seen, refers to man's communicability. What they are predicting (if that is the right word) is a communion between men which is deeper, closer and stonger than anything we normally experience.

Nor do Paul and the psalmist envisage this as happening in some other world. The biblical hope is for a resurrection of the world we know, and of the people in it. To speak of the resurrection of the body is to speak of the sharing by all men in the future of mankind and in the world we live in.

The difficulty we have in coping with this idea stems from our western individualism. We are used to thinking in terms of "my" soul, "my" salvation, "my" union with God. The biblical hope is not so self-centered. Salvation is to be bodily.

And if the body is the way in which we are related to each other, then the final resurrection of the body cannot be said to have been achieved until all men are fully related to each other. We cannot speak of our own bodily resurrection without including the resurrection of all men, indeed of the whole universe. We cannot profess our faith in the resurrection of the body without hoping to be embodied in each other. And insofar as we already have some experience of this here and now, the resurrection of the body has begun, and in fact is going on all the time.

The Nicaraguan poet Ernesto Cardenal has published some reflections along these lines:

> Nature is constantly communing with itself. It is always eating itself and offering itself to be eaten. Food is the communion of life. Food is not 'prosaic.' The Creator willed that in order to live we must eat other living beings because he wanted living beings to be in communion with one another . . . [and] with the whole cosmos. . . . With what body shall we rise? We shall rise with all bodies and all ages, or rather one single body will rise again, with many ages. In it we shall all be flesh of others and within one another as the foetus is in its mother. . . .
>
> That is why our religion is catholic, that is to say, universal, not just because it is the religion of all men but because it is the religion of the whole cosmos. It reaches from molluscs to the stars . . . .
>
> These worlds are dumb. They praise God, but with unconscious praise. They do not know they are doing it. And you are the voice of these worlds and their awareness. But these worlds are not capable of love, whereas you are.
>
> But your mind is not separate from these worlds. You are also this vast universe. You are its mind and heart. You are the vast universe thinking and loving . . .
>
> The whole universe is really a single mass of matter, more or less rarefied or concentrated and the whole cosmos is a single body. . . . So we are made of star, or rather the cosmos is made of our own flesh.

> And when the Word was made flesh and dwelt among
> us, he could have said of all nature, as Adam said of
> Eve: "This now is flesh of my flesh and bone of my
> bones." In Christ's body, as in ours, there is all creation
> (*Love*, Search Press, London 1974, pp. 137–42).

Cardenal's thought owes not a little to the renewed interest of the West in eastern philosophy, especially in Zen Buddhism, whose deep abhorrence of any dualistic division between matter and spirit gives it a close affinity with the biblical thought we have been discussing. In an article, acclaimed by Buddhists as containing more true understanding of Zen than anything written by a western writer, the Catholic monk Thomas Merton reproached us for the ease with which we can say, "I am aware of x y z," when in reality that awareness is in no way mine as a private possession. The truth is that *being* aware of itself in me, that the whole universe, as a totality, is aware of itself in me.

> 'I' am not limited to my individual and empirical self,
> still less to a disembodied soul . . . My 'identity' is to
> be sought not in that *separation* from all that is, but
> in *oneness* with all that is (*The Zen Revival*, Buddhist
> Society, London, p. 8).

Perhaps some Buddhists are more open to an understanding of the biblical doctrine of the bodily resurrection than some Christians are:

THE BODY OF CHRIST

Let me sum up what I have said in this chapter by recalling a recent experience. A number of my students were trying to learn a little about the communication media by offering themselves for interview before a television camera, and then watching a playback so that they could judge for themselves how well they had done.

We discussed the experience afterwards. Most of us were deeply embarrassed by the completely new angle we had been given on our own body. It seemed to us more of an encumbrance than a help. Face, speech, hands, gestures, even the brain — all seemed to be made of wood. The shyness and self-consciousness we had felt before the camera paled into insignificance before the wretched image the playback presented to us. We yearned to be disburdened of this clumsy medium, which apparently could do no more than stand in the way of any real communication between souls.

We reflected further, and came to the conclusion, not without reluctance, that for all our misgivings the body was the only medium we had for communicating with each other. Eyes, mouth and hands may be cumbersome, but they are the only bridge across which we can make contact with others. In fact they are the very expression of our communion with each other; without them we would remain closed in on ourselves, incommunicado. The problem was not that we were too human, too bodily; we were not bodily and human enough. Our body was only partially functioning, and what we were really yearning for was a body which did perfectly what a body was designed to do.

The Christian believes that this yearning was answered at the first Easter. To say that Jesus has been raised is to say that his body has been perfected, and that he is now able powerfully to share himself with all men. And to say that we form part of that body, the Corpus Christi, is to claim that the same transformation has begun in us. The Christian is committed to the faith that God does not make contact with us in the abstract, but in the earthly and bodily, with all the ambiguity that such a mediated contact implies.

The story is told of a Pakistani immigrant to Britain who was dying of a kidney complaint. His heart was still sound and he was asked to donate it. He agreed on condition that before he died he could be taken to see the beneficiary. A visit was arranged and the purpose of it explained to the rather surprised recipient, who had difficulty in grasping why a coloured man was visiting him. "O, thank God," he said when he finally understood, "I thought he was coming to live next door."

The story serves as a parable of the Christian reality. The Christian believes in a man who was not merely tolerated as an undesirable alien, but whom some of his contemporaries were determined to kill; who came to live not merely next door, but in our own home; whose gaze meets us day after day, out of the eyes of those with whom he claimed to be identified. The Christian is committed to something as bodily as that.

Chapter Six

The Resurrection and Peter

In the course of a seminar, I was trying desperately to get the group to volunteer the information that in the gospel accounts of the resurrrection Peter has a prominent role to play.[1] None of the group had apparently noticed this, and I tried to inject the information as unobtrusively as possible. When my cautious efforts finally registered, they were immediately challenged by a nun. Her recollection was that Peter's name only occurred once, and then only as an aside, in the Emmaus story: the two disciples return from the country to be told that "the Lord has appeared to Simon." True, her name was Magdalene,

---

[1]This chapter is not meant to be an *apologia* for the Roman primacy: the connection of the Roman See with Peter is a secondary question in which the New Testament shows no interest. My concern is with the place ascribed to Peter by the New Testament, especially in its resurrection accounts. No distinction is made here between the various names given him in the text, whether it be Peter, or Simon, or Simon Peter, or Cephas.

and she may have been distantly conscious of the fact that in other traditions it is Mary of Magdala who was the first to see the risen Christ. Still, it had not occurred to her that the point of the Emmaus story ending is that, cock-a-hoop as the visionaries are with their tale of meeting Christ, the wind is taken out of their sails by the announcement that while they were away *Peter* had already seen him (Luke 24:34).

FIRST TO CEPHAS

In actual fact, that is not the only text which singles out Peter as the first witness of the resurrection. (The previous appearance to Mary of Magdala, with or without companions, does not in fact invalidate this use of the word "first"; in the ethos of the time, regrettable as this may have been, a woman could not act as an official witness.) *Peter* is also mentioned as the first to have seen the risen Christ in a tradition which Paul quotes as having been in existence before the year AD 45 when he began his ministry:

> I taught you what I had been taught myself, namely that Christ . . . was raised to life on the third day, in accordance with the scriptures; that he appeared first to Cephas and secondly to the Twelve (1 Corinthians 15:3–5).

Here Peter is not only named first in a list which puts Paul chronologically last, but he is explicitly specified as "first."

Luke, who has no preliminary women's vision of Christ as the other evangelists have, tells a story (in a text which is admittedly less certain than the rest) of *Peter* being the first of the disciples to rush to the tomb to find it empty, and of his amazement (Luke 24:12). Taken in conjunction with the end of the Emmaus story the text, if it is genuine, expresses the ambiguous nature of the Easter event: Peter both saw nothing and was the first to "see" the risen Christ.

But Luke's story may simply be a reflection of John's, where *Peter* is the first to enter the tomb, even though the "disciple whom Jesus loved" had arrived before him. In John, this story has been deliberately inserted into the Magdalene story. It interrupts the account of her vision of Christ, in order somehow to establish Peter's prior claim to an understanding of the resurrection (John 20:3–10).

This series of texts is impressive. In spite of the existence of other traditions, and in spite of the constant reminder that the women really saw him first (Mark's appendix specifies Mary of Magdala as "first" in as emphatic a way as Paul specifies Peter, Mark 16:9), Peter remains prominent in tradition as the first witness of the resurrection.

Principal References to Peter in the New Testament

Searches for Jesus after he had risen. Mark 1:35–39.
First to be told of the resurrection. Mark 16:7 & 9, John 20:2
First to find the tomb empty. Luke 24:12.
First to enter the tomb. John 20:3–10.
First to see the risen Christ. Luke 24:34, 1 Corinthians 15:5.
First in lists of the apostles. Mark 3:16, Matthew 10:2, Luke 6:14.
First of the disciples called. Mark 1:17, Matthew 4:19, Luke 5:10.
Fisher of men like Jesus. Luke 5:10.
Shepherd of Jesus' flock. John 21:15–17.
Walks on the water with Jesus. Matthew 14:28, John 21:7.
Professes Jesus as the Holy One of God. John 6:68.
Professes Jesus as the Christ. Mark 8:29, Matthew 16:16, Luke 9:20.
Foundation stone of his brethren's faith. Matthew 16:18; John 1:42, Luke 22:31.
Preacher of forgiveness. Matthew 16:19.
Spokesman at Jesus' appearance. Mark 9:5, Matthew 17:4, Luke 9:33.
Spokesman for the disciples. Gospels and Acts *passim*.
Source of tradition about Jesus. Galatians 1:18.

GO AND TELL PETER

There are other texts which echo this emphasis on Peter's part of the resurrection story. The most explicit is the one which ends Mark's gospel, where the women, stupefied by the message of the angel, register sufficiently to understand that they must pass this message on "to his disciples *and to Peter*" (Mark 16:7). The meaning is "above all to Peter." The reader is being sent back to the prediction earlier in the same gospel that Jesus would in the end be deserted by his disciples, above all by the boastful and self-confident Peter (Mark 14:27–31). The first to abandon Jesus is singled out as the first to hear of his resurrection.

In John's resurrection narrative also, where the tomb is discovered empty by Mary of Magdala, it is not the disciples in general to whom she first breaks the news but *Peter* (John 20:2). In one of the sequels to Mark's gospel, the vision of the angel is similarly reported "to those with *Peter*." This sequel, known as the "shorter ending," is no more part of Mark's original gospel than the "longer ending" which appears in our Bibles, but it does produce further evidence of the conviction in the minds of the first generation of Christians that in the resurrection story Peter somehow stands in the forefront.

SIMON PETER JUMPED

We have looked so far at the explicit resurrection narratives. But the whole gospel from beginning to end is an implicit resurrection narrative. All its stories have been influenced by the subsequent fact of Easter, and are designed to present to the reader not a dead Jesus of the past, but the risen Christ of the present. We must search those stories too, especially those which contain clear echoes of the resurrection, to discover the part which the New Testament assigns to Peter.

Mark, as we have seen, tells of the resurrection without feeling the need to narrate any appearances of the risen Christ. In his gospel, the place of these seems to be taken by the dazzling appearance of Jesus at the transfiguration, where a voice from heaven gives him the title which Christians took up after Easter, "Son of God." It is interesting, therefore, that in this scene too *Peter* should again have a certain prominence. It is he who speaks for his awestruck companions to express the wish that the present experience could last forever (Mark 9:2–8).

The story of the walking on the water (Matthew 14:22–23 and parallels) has long been recognized as a close relative of the resurrection stories. To begin with, the water over which Jesus shows his mastery is a natural symbol, in biblical thought, of the death which devours all other men. The story itself is told in terms of the disciples' fear, their uncertainty about whether they are seeing a ghost, the reassurance "Do not be afraid: it is I," and the recognition of the "Lord." These words are clearly meant to echo the resurrection accounts, where precisely the same terms are used to describe the disciples' reaction to the appearance of the risen Christ (see for instance Luke 24:35, 37, 38, 39).

When Matthew and John tell the story (Matthew 14:28, John 21:7), *Peter* is invited to share Jesus' experience of walking on the water. Even though it is the "other disciple" who first recognizes the stranger as the Lord, it is Peter who jumps, and discovers, not without floundering, that by taking Jesus' hand the "impossible" becomes possible for him too. He too is able to share Jesus' mastery over the death-dealing elements.

Matthew and John both conclude the story with a profession of the disciples' faith, "Truly, you are the Son of God" (Matthew 14:33); "You are the Holy One of God" (John 6:68). The latter is explicitly attributed to *Peter*. Through Peter's almost disastrous experience, he and his brethren recognize Jesus, and give him the titles which Christians later gave to the risen Christ.

This profession of faith in Jesus as the God-sent savior of his people is a turning point in the gospel of John. Mark relegates the confession to a later chapter because he too wants it to form the center of his gospel, and is in fact most careful to omit the professions of faith with which the other evangelists punctuate their text, so that his story can reach a climax with the words, "You are the Christ, the Messiah" (Mark 8:29). It is significant therefore that this profession of faith is again attributed to *Peter*. True, Peter is almost immediately reprimanded for his inadequate understanding of the title (Mark 8:33). Nonetheless the tradition is firm — and it is repeated by Matthew and Luke — that Peter was the first of the disciples to recognize Jesus as Messiah. In Matthew's telling of the story, Jesus solemnly pronounces that on this profession of faith the Christian community would be founded (Matthew 16:13–18).

It is not surprising, therefore, to find a strong tradition that *Peter* was the first of the disciples to be called by Jesus (Mark 1:17, Matthew 4:19, Luke 5:10), in spite of the fact that other traditions do not agree that this was so (John 1:35–42 gives priority to two of the Baptist's disciples). Mark, in relating this tradition, follows it up with lines which have strange overtones of the resurrection about them, especially as Mark himself narrates it; and here too *Peter* has a place: "Very early in the morning, having risen, he (Jesus) . . . went off to a lonely place . . . Simon and his companions set out in search of him, and when they found him they said, 'Everybody is looking for you' . . . And he went through Galilee"(Mark 1:35–39).

The prominence these texts give to Peter corresponds to the leading role which the rest of the New Testament attributes to him. Where he is mentioned in the epistles of Paul, he is to be one of the principal sources of tradition about Jesus (Galatians 1:18). In the Acts of the Apostles he dominates the whole of the first half of the story of the spread of Christianity. In the gospels he is the first named in all the lists of the apostles (Mark 3:16, Luke 6:14. Matthew 10:2 not only names him first but specifies him, as Paul's resurrection account did, as "the first"). Throughout the gospels he appears as spokesman for his companions, the shepherd of the "little flock," and the prototype of the disciple who would take up Jesus' own mission as a fisher of men.

95

ON THIS ROCK I WILL BUILD

What can we conclude from this series of texts? The New Testament has gone out of its way, it would seem to put Peter in the forefront, first in the resurrection stories, and subsequently in portraying the position he held among his fellow disciples, as their spokesman and confessor of their Easter faith. Why?

The implication is that Peter's primacy consists precisely in his resurrection-faith. To put it in plainer terms, Peter was the first to "see" the risen Christ, that is to say, to experience Jesus as alive after the tragedy of Calvary; and the Christian community acknowledged that their "seeing" of Jesus was dependent on Peter's.

This is not to say that Peter's fantasy or wish-fulfilment became theirs. We are speaking of an experience of a Jesus who was alive in reality, not merely in their imagination. But the resurrection was not proclaimed until Peter came to believe this. Unless Peter had made this venture of faith first, and discovered the living Jesus who was there to be discovered, his fellow disciples would not have discovered him for themselves. Peter's faith led others to faith. The mission of the Church is based on Peter's vision and insight.

Two stories in particular underline this. The first is the story of the walking on the water (Matthew 14:28), to which I have already referred. Jesus had invited Peter to come, to discover that he could do what Jesus did. Just as he had been promised that he would be a fisher of men as Jesus was (Luke 5:10), and that he would be able to cast out devils as Jesus did (Matthew 10:1), so he was invited to have a faith like that of Jesus, and to master with him the waters of death. By making such a venture of faith, even if hesitantly at first, *Peter* discovered that the Jesus with whom he walked the waters was indeed alive. And his recovery of faith at that crucial moment was the condition on which all his fellow disciples discovered Jesus as the Lord.

The second story is even more telling. Luke recounts Jesus' prediction of Peter's denial in the context of a prayer that *Peter's* faith would not finally fail, because it was to be the

96

foundation of his brethren's faith. Only a Peter turning from disbelief to faith could be a source of strength to his fellow disciples (Luke 22:31–34).

WHOSE SINS YOU FORGIVE

How exactly did Peter arrive at the conviction that Jesus was alive after his death? What precisely was the insight on which he based his Easter faith? The New Testament does not tell us the answer to this question, but it does give us some hints.

John tells the story of the risen Christ's first appearance to his assembled brethren. In view of their recent behavior, they might have expected his first words to be: "Where in God's name did you all get to? Fine friends you showed yourselves to be! The first sign of trouble, and all I could see was your heels!" Instead, says the story, the first words they heard him say were: "Shalom, peace." They expected a reprimand; their first experience was of the risen Christ's forgiveness.

The story immediately elaborates the theme by representing Jesus showing the disciples his wounded hands and side, and saying: "As the Father sent me, so I am sending you. Receive the Holy Spirit. For those whose sins you forgive, they are forgiven" (John 20:19–22). Jesus' own reaction to his sufferings, they are given to understand, is to forgive. To pay back evil for evil can only make evil grow by geometrical progression. To absorb it by forgiveness is the only way to make it disappear. It is a costly process, and if the disciples wish to follow the example of Jesus they will be wounded as Jesus was. But in the spirit of Jesus they are being sent out to do what Jesus did.

In short, the context in which the disciples first saw the risen Jesus was one of forgiveness. And this would come home above all to *Peter*. According to the gospel tradition, he not only deserted Jesus in his hour of need, but denied him three times. The realization that such treachery was not unforgivable, and was in fact forgiven, must have been for him an overwhelming experience.

Peter as the forgiven disciple is in fact the theme of a whole number of gospel stories. It is he who protests over having his feet washed by Jesus, and then realizes that he needs washing all over (John 13:9). It is he who breaks down in uncontrollable tears when his eyes meet the eyes of his forgiving master (Luke 22:61–62). It is he who is singled out as able to proclaim the resurrection precisely because he denied Jesus (Mark 16:7, see 14:29). It is he who makes amends for this threefold denial by the threefold declaration of his love for Jesus, and thereby becomes shepherd of the flock (John 21:15–17). It is he whose profession of faith in Jesus as Son of the living God is immediately followed by the charge to forgive, for whatever he refuses to forgive heaven itself cannot forgive (Matthew 16:19). Indeed, it is this "power of the keys," of which Peter had first become conscious, which the whole community must eventually shoulder (Matthew 18:18). Only through their forgiveness could they become a sacrament of Jesus to the world, a sign to men that the risen Christ was still active in their midst.

Peter, then, is a symbol of the Christian disciple. In a sense, he is the embodiment of the communal failure of all his brethren, just as he is the spokesman of their communal faith. He is man in his weakness and sinfulness, again and again misunderstanding the Christian message and earning the rebuke of Jesus, whom he finally even denies. But he is also the man who repents, who cries out to be saved, and in that moment is snatched from disaster. The man of little faith stretches out his hand to Jesus, and finds him ever living and ever forgiving.

But this communal understanding of the gospel could not be achieved until someone had lived through it, and the whole New Testament bears witness that this someone was Peter. His experience of the risen Christ's forgiveness was decisive, and his faith was constitutive of the Church. Peter thinking the things of man is a stumbling block, but Peter thinking the things of God is a rock on which the Christian community can be built (Matthew 16:17–23).

For the Christian Church is nothing (as my opening quotation from St. Paul stressed) if it does not believe in the resurrection, that is to say, if it does not show by its action that it is committed to a forgiving Christ who lives on beyond death. As a recent scholar has put it, "There is no hope of understanding the resurrection outside the process of renewing humanity in forgiveness. We are all agreed that the empty tomb proves nothing; we need to add that no amount of apparitions, however well authenticated, would mean anything either apart from the testimony of forgiven lives communicating forgiveness" (Rowan Williams, *Resurrection*, Darton Longman & Todd, London, 1982, p. 118).

CHAPTER SEVEN

Difficulties Remaining

The title of this book ends with a question mark. It is meant to suggest that the conclusions I have arrived at, however pungently presented, are only tentative. I genuinely wish to remain an asker of questions about the resurrection, not to pose as a solver of all its problems.

If this is true of the book as a whole, it is even more true of this chapter. Here I am not only asking questions: I cannot even propose any very satisfactory answers. But I would like to put the questions all the same, lest I should be thought to have evaded some of the difficulties which, when all is said and done, still remain.

THE EMPTY TOMB

It was suggested above in Chapter 2 that the story of the empty tomb was in large part an "objectivization," a presentation in a concrete form of a reality which itself has nothing to do with what can or cannot be seen in a cemetery. But what actually happened to the tomb of Jesus? Was it miraculously emptied, or is it possible that archaeologists will one day find the remains of Jesus still there?

Many Christian scholars agree that the answer to this question would make no difference to the resurrection itself, since this is a reality of an entirely different order from that supposed by the question. But if the empty tomb *is* only part of the story, however expressive of that deeper reality the story may be, what actually happened to the body?

If "body" means the flesh and blood which cannot inherit the Kingdom of God, then one would have to say that it turned to dust, as ours will. But if "body" means (more accurately) that by which the individual Jesus is related to his brethren, one would have to say that it "became" the Christian community and that this is why the community is called the "Body of Christ."

Does such an explanation sufficiently safeguard Jesus' distinctness from the Christian community? Is there not a sense in which his separate identity as an individual needs to be maintained? If he continues to live "only" in his community, then what is the difference between saying "Jesus lives on" and saying, for instance, (as posters all over Russia say) "Lenin lived, Lenin lives on, Lenin will live"? Is it simply that Christians have discovered that Jesus lives on in a way others do not, that he lives on *for them*? But in that case, is not the uniqueness of Christ reduced to something merely relative?

THE APPEARANCES

If the "seeing" of the risen Christ reported by the gospels is not a physical reality but, like the story of the empty tomb, the "objectivization" of an interior vision, then why draw up a list of witnesses? If "I have seen the risen Christ" means no more than "I believe in the resurrection," is not every believer a "seer" of the risen Christ? Then why bother to mention the "five hundred of the brothers at the same time" (1 Corinthians 15:6) as if their vision was something exceptional?

The difficulty must have been felt from the earliest times because, in spite of the fact that the "appearances" had

101

traditionally ended after forty days, Paul insists in this text that his vision of the risen Christ years later is quite as valid as the earlier ones. Yet if this is so, why does he mention his own vision as "the last"? Is not my seeing of the risen Christ today as valid as his? How can there ever be a last?

Obviously there was something distinctive about the first witnesses of the resurrection. They alone were able to provide the link between their resurrection experience and the historical Jesus, to verify that what they saw now was in the strictest continuity with what they had seen before. In this sense their "seeing" of the risen Christ was foundational, and every later act of faith in the resurrection is based on their witness. However, the difficulty raised by Paul's use of the words "last of all" remains. He had not seen the historical Jesus — he even boasts of the fact in 2 Corinthians 5:16. Why include his vision in the list and not mine? Was he the exception that proves the rule? Was that why he felt impelled to preach to the Gentiles, who were in exactly the same position as himself?

JERUSALEM AND GALILEE

I pointed out in Chapter 3 that the gospel accounts do not agree about the location of the resurrection events. Matthew and Mark place the appearance(s) of Christ in Galilee, Luke John in Jerusalem. Where did these events take place in reality?

Did the original preaching of the gospel omit place-names as irrelevant, since the important thing is that Jesus lives on after death among his disciples wherever they may happen to be? Certainly Paul's famous list of appearances does not bother to mention where these were supposed to have taken place. Obviously whoever was granted a vision must have been somewhere. But where does not seem to have mattered as much as it does to us, with our subconscious picture of a revivified corpse travelling from place to place.

Did the evangelists simply supply whatever location fitted in best with their own interests, so that Matthew chose Galilee because he envisaged its hill-country as a new Mount Sinai, and Luke chose Jerusalem because he saw the Jewish capital as the center of salvation? Or did Luke quite deliberately omit the Galilee appearances (suggests a bright amateur) so as not to confuse readers?

Or did the first appearances in actual historical fact take place in Galilee, where the disciples would naturally have returned after the Passover feast (this is the conclusion of most scholars), and was the location only moved to Jerusalem because that eventually became the center of Christianity?

But this raises the further question of how exactly faith in the resurrection originated. I indicated in Chapter 6 that Peter's own understanding of the resurrection seems to have been crucial: the community's faith in the risen Christ was dependent on his. But if Peter's faith was insight rather than physical vision, does the emphasis on the part played by the Jerusalem women suggest that even his official witness was dependent on their "unoffical" report that Jesus was alive? Was it they who really first "saw" the risen Christ, and did Peter come to his experience of the resurrection only subsequently?

Or is the story of Jesus appearing to the women only a later elaboration of the original gospel story in which it is an *angel* who appears to the women, an angel who is already beginning to speak with the voice of Jesus in Matthew 28:7b?

ON THE THIRD DAY

If, in Karl Rahner's phrase, Jesus' resurrection is not another event after his death but simply the manifestation of what happened when Jesus died, then it is difficult to understand why the New Testament places such emphasis on "the third day." If Jesus' death *is* already the resurrection (and indeed, according to John and Luke, the ascension too), why are these last presented as if they were separate events, one after three days according to the gospels, and the other after another forty days according to the Acts of the Apostles? Is it that Luke in writing his gospel is deliberately being the theologian, while in writing his Acts he is attempting a presentation which has a more historical air about it? What precisely is supposed to have happened on the third day? Simply the appearance(s) of Jesus, as distinct from his actual resurrection? But then why does the text of the New Testament keep repeating the words "*raised* on the third day"?

Is the expression "the third day," as some suggest, a hebrewism to indicate a short and indefinite period of time (there is a little, but very little evidence for this)? Or is it, as others hold, a reflection of the belief that the body does not begin to corrupt until after the third day when the soul departs? But could Jewish writers such as the evangelists were entertain so physicalist and dualist a view? Or is the expression based on the Talmudic teaching that the general resurrection of all men would begin on the third day after the end of the world? If so, then the phrase would equivalently be a claim that in Jesus' resurrection a new world has dawned.

What precise Old Testament text do the gospels have in mind when they refer to the "the third day" as foretold in the scriptures? The words of Hosea are often quoted:

> Let us return to the Lord.
> He has torn us to pieces, but he will heal us . . .
> on the third day he will raise us (6:1–2)

but the fortuitous association of "third day" and "raise" scarcely adds up to a prediction of the resurrection, especially when one realizes that the prophet is here upbraiding his people for presuming on God's healing. Some scholars suggest that "three days" is a traditional scriptural way of referring to God's intervention after near disaster, and they quote in confirmation the sacrifice of Isaac (Genesis 22:4), the release of Joseph's brothers from prison (Genesis 42:18), the appearance of Yahweh at Sinai (Exodus 19:16), the appointment of David as king (2 Samuel 1:2), Hezekiah's recovery from sickness (2 Kings 20:5), Esther's salvation of her people (Esther 5:1) and Jonah's escape from the whale (Jonah 2:1 — this text is actually quoted in Matthew 12:40). But these examples are rather arbitrarily chosen, and others could be found where the third day is the day of disaster, or where God's intervention comes after a longer or shorter period of time.

Is it possible that the New Testament is not claiming that the third day was foretold at all, but only the resurrection itself, at least in the sense of suffering transformed into joy? Should our translations perhaps be corrected, so that they no longer read, "On the third day, as scripture foretold, he was raised from the dead," but "On the third day he was, as scripture foretold, raised from the dead"?

Many more questions could be asked, and no doubt will be, about this detail of the resurrection story and others. These will suffice to assure the reader that the explanation of the resurrection given in these pages is only one of many. If I have protested about those who would impose their explanation as the only orthodox one, it would be strange if I tried to impose mine.

Postscript

When I spent a sabbatical term at the *École Biblique* in Jerusalem, the BBC asked me to visit some of the most popular Christian shrines in the locality, and to record my impressions *in situ*. Since these broadcasts touch on many of the themes dealt with in this book — the secular reality of Jesus, the indivisibility of his death and resurrection, the outpouring of his Spirit on his disciples and the formation of them into his risen Body — I include the text here as a postscript.

The broadcasts were preceded by a reading of the appropriate gospel text.

BETHLEHEM

> Joseph set out from the town of Nazareth in Galilee and travelled up to Judaea, to the town of David called Bethlehem, since he was of David's House and line, in order to be registered with Mary, his

betrothed, who was with child. While they were there the time came for her to have her child and she gave birth to a son, her first-born. She wrapped him in swaddling clothes and laid him in a manger because there was no room for them at the inn.

In the countryside close by there were shepherds who lived in the fields and took it in turns to watch their flocks during the night. The angel of the Lord appeared to them and the glory of the Lord shone round them. They were terrified, but the angel said, "Do not be afraid. Listen, I bring you news of great joy, a joy to be shared by the whole people. Today in the town of David a savior has been born to you; he is Christ the Lord. And here is a sign for you: you will find a baby wrapped in swaddling clothes and lying in a manger" (Luke 2:4–12).

As you come into the little town of Bethlehem, and it's from there I'm talking to you, you are greeted by a large banner across the road which reads, in Hebrew, "Beruchim Habaim — Blessed is he who comes"; and underneath it, in Arabic, "Ahalan vesahalan — My tent is yours." It's a great joy to be welcomed so gracefully to one's ancestral home. Because coming to Bethlehem as a Christian, you have the feeling of going back to your roots.

The great basilica of the Nativity, as it's called, stands in the center of the town. It was built more than 1600 years ago over the cave which the early Christians venerated as the place where Jesus was born. The roofing that I see as I look up is, they say, English oak, donated by King Edward III at a time when the church was in need of restoration. The Crusaders who rescued the church from the Saracens walled up the doors to stop soldiers riding in on horseback, and for centuries the only entrance to the vast interior has been a tiny postern gate, where you have to bend double, almost, to avoid banging your head.

At the far end of the church in which I'm standing, some steps cut into the rock go down into the cave, and here too you have to stoop quite low until you stand in the cave, and look at

107

the silver star set into the ground and the inscription, "Here, of the Virgin Mary, was born Jesus Christ."

It's a sort of parable, I've always thought when I've visited Bethlehem, that no one can come and see the place where Jesus was born without making this act of humility and obeisance. It's as if the very stones are saying to you, "You've got to stoop here, pilgrim, this place where God has stooped so low for you."

Because it's a very strange thing that we have to preach to the world, those of us who believe in Christ: that God is no longer to be looked for where people *do* look for him, up there, out yonder, up in the heavens — only here, in something as utterly human as the birth of a child. "But that doesn't look like God" we can hear ourselves saying, and the reply comes back, "Who knows what God looks like?" "Well this is nothing like my idea of God" we say, and the reply is, "Very likely; and it's your idea of God which has to go."

The birth of Christ, for those who believe in him, means that from this moment on, the indescribable mystery which we call God can only be found in someone entirely like you and me. What the Christian is really trying to say at Christmas is, "I believe in Man."

The first people who heard this strange teaching called it atheism. "This," they said, "is emptying the heavens and getting rid of the gods. Away with these godless people," they said. I sometimes wonder whether those first persecutions haven't given us Christians a sort of subconscious phobia, so that we've been scared ever since to say openly what our origins here at Bethlehem proclaim, that we believe in Man.

DOMINUS FLEVIT

As Jesus drew near and came in sight of the city he shed tears over it and said, "If you in your turn had only understood on this day the message of peace! But, alas, it is hidden from your eyes! Yes, a time is coming when your enemies will raise fortifications all around you, when they will encircle you and hem you in on every side; they will dash you and the children

> inside your walls to the ground; they will leave not
> one stone standing on another within you — and all
> because you did not recognize your opportunity
> when God offered it!"
>
> When some were talking about the Temple,
> remarking how it was adorned with fine stonework
> and votive offerings, he said, "All these things you
> are staring at now — the time will come when not a
> single stone will be left on another: everything will be de-
> stroyed" (Luke 19:41-4; 21:5-6).

I'm standing in one of my favorite spots in Jerusalem. Well,
outside Jerusalem really, on the Mount of Olives. But it allows
you to see, as no other place in Jerusalem does, the whole town
in one magnificent panorama, especially at this time of day,
when the morning sun is shining straight on the city walls
which run along the crest of the hill opposite, and beyond,
lighting up the great golden dome of the Mosque which now
stands where the temple used to stand.

Halfway up the olive-groved hill on this side of the
valley, a chapel has stood since Byzantine times to commemo-
rate the episode in the gospel story where the disciples of Jesus
were admiring the view, as I am now. "Look at the temple,"
they were saying, "look at those magnificent stones, look at
those wonderful buildings." and Jesus, says the evangelist,
wept. The chapel is called *Dominus Flevit,* The Lord Wept.

He was weeping, as any good Jew would, at the pros-
pect of those magnificent stones and wonderful buildings
being destroyed. Anyone with his finger on the political pulse
of those times could see that Jewish opposition to the Roman
occupation could only end in one way, which it did forty years
later. Not one stone, as Jesus had forecast, was left on another.

But Jesus would be weeping, too, over the conviction
growing in him that what he had undertaken in his preaching
was a one-man-stand against a whole system and all that it
stood for. And that too could only end in one way.

I've often stood here, as I'm doing now, looking across
the valley at the temple area, and thought about what it stood
for in the time of Jesus. It stood for Abraham, at the very dawn

of history, people said, and the willingness he showed to sacrifice his only son Isaac on that hill. It stood for King David, and all the energy he devoted to making that hill into his capital city. It stood for Solomon in all his glory, who built the first temple over there to mark that hill as the meeting place of God and men.

It stood for the desolation of a whole nation when that temple was destroyed, and all Jerusalem was carried off into exile by the rivers of Babylon. It stood for the super-human efforts of those who returned to build the temple again on the same hill. It stood for the thousands upon thousands of Jewish pilgrims who came to that temple over the next five hundred years, singing the psalms we still use today. It stood for the lavish building project which King Herod had undertaken just fifty years before Jesus wept, to turn that temple into one of the wonders of the ancient world.

All that is what the temple stood for as Jesus looked at it from the hillside. In the light of all that, we may think, what a fantastic claim for him to come along and say, "You can pull it all down; I'll take over." And yet someone needs to have the courage to say that from time to time about any temple, or religious institution or system, which is beginning to exist for its own sake, and about which people have forgotten to ask, "What's it all for?"

It's all for man. The place where God meets men is not in holy buildings or systems or institutions, but in their own lives. And if the only way you can demonstrate that is by giving your life, then you weep, but you know it's got to be done.

CENACLE

> As they were at table, Jesus took some bread, and when he had given thanks, broke it and gave it to them, saying, "This is my body which will be given for you; do this as a memorial of me . . . "
>
> Then Jesus got up from the table, removed his outer garment and, taking a towel, wrapped it round his waist; he then poured water into a basin and began to wash the disciples' feet and to wipe them with the towel he was wearing . . .

When he had washed their feet and put on his
clothes again he went back to the table. "Do you
understand" he said, "what I have done to you? . . . I
have given you an example so that you may copy
what I have done to you . . .
   I give you a new commandment:
   love one another . . .
   By this love you have for one another,
   everyone will know that you are my disciples"
(Luke 22:19; John 13:4– 35).

Up here on the western slope of "old" Jerusalem, at the very
opposite end from where I was speaking yesterday, there's a
place which Christians have venerated for 1500 years as the
Upper Room. The room is mentioned twice in the gospels, once
as the place where Jesus ate his last supper with his disciples,
and then later as the place where the disciples, huddled
together after the bewildering events of Good Friday and
Easter, were bowled over, the New Testament says, by the
experience of finding themselves filled with the Spirit of the
risen Christ, and went out preaching the marvels of God to
anyone who cared to listen. It was the first Whit Sunday.

   Today the Upper Room is not much more than just
that, an empty room one floor up in an empty house. The
pillars holding up the ceiling date from Crusader times, but
otherwise there's nothing to see here. For many years the
building stood right on the frontier between the embattled
Israelis and Arabs, and not many pilgrims found their way
here. But even today, when the border has disappeared and it's
open again to all comers, you see very few Christians up here.
In fact, the place has far more Jewish visitors than Christians,
because downstairs, across that courtyard, here in the only
corner of "old" Jerusalem that Jews had access to until
recently, they keep the memory of King David (he's said to be
buried there); and alongside his grave they keep the memory of
the millions upon millions of Jews who were buried in mass
graves after being rounded up, starved, stripped and gassed in
Dachau, Belsen, Auschwitz, and the other Nazi concentration
camps of the 30s and 40s.

111

What a shattering thought that these two places should be so close together, one on top of the other: the Christian Upper Room with its memories of the eucharist and of Pentacost (Whitsun we call it, White Sunday); and the Jewish Lower Room with its walls and ceilings black with the smoke of candles burning in memory of a holocaust.

This room up here with its echoes of Jesus' last meal with his disciples, and his words as he gave them the passover bread, "This is my body"; and that room downstairs where they still exhibit a jar containing a piece of soap with a Nazi label proclaiming it's made from the bones of a concentration camp victim. What poor Jew has to point at that jar and say, "This is my body"?

This room up here where Christians over the centuries have recalled the unforgettable words of Jesus as he went to his passion, that the way you'd be able to tell followers of his was by the love they had for their brothers and the service they were willing to do them; and that room down there with its damning evidence of the travesty we made of those words in the Christian West as we sent six million of our brothers to their passion.

Those of us who claim we weren't directly responsible, do we think that we're excused by the fact that we looked the other way saying, "Who is my brother?" Spirit of Jesus, I have to say as I stand in this Upper Room, come and breathe some warmth into the chilled hearts of your disciples, and me first of all.

GETHSEMANE

Jesus made his way as usual to the Mount of Olives, with the disciples following. When they reached the place he said to them, "Pray not to be put to the test." Then he withdrew from them, about a stone's throw away, and knelt down and prayed. "Father," he said, "if you are willing, take this cup away from me. Nevertheless, let your will be done, not mine" . . . In his anguish he prayed even more earnestly, and his sweat fell to the ground like great drops of blood . . .

God did not appoint angels to be rulers of the world to come, but a man. . . . It is not as if we had a high priest who was incapable of feeling our weaknesses with us; we have one who has been tempted in every way that we are. . . . And so he can sympathize with those who are ignorant or uncertain because he too lives in the limitations of weakness. . . .

During his life on earth, he offered up prayer and entreaty, aloud and in silent tears, to the one who had the power to save him out of death, and he submitted so humbly that his prayer was heard. . . . Let us not lose sight of Jesus, who leads us in our faith (Luke 22:39–44, Hebrews 2:5–12:2).

Between the Mount of Olives where I was on Tuesday, and the Upper Room from which I spoke to you yesterday, runs the Kidron valley. On the floor of that valley lies the garden of Gethsemane, where the gospels tell us Jesus spent his last night before he was arrested, tried and put to death.

The evangelist says that he used it often as a place to bring his disciples to. The Franciscan fathers who have had charge of the place over the centuries have tended it with loving care: you won't see flowers as beautiful or as fragrant as the ones I'm now admiring anywhere else in Jerusalem. The flower-beds are shaded from the sun by olive trees, gnarled and twisted, several hundred years old, the great-great-grandsons, I should think, of the trees Jesus and his disciples knew.

Behind me stands the "Basilica of all Nations," as it's called. During the 1930s everyone wanted to contribute towards rebuilding the church which has been here since the fourth century, and all the Christian nations are remembered inside on the ceiling, where their flags are displayed in mosaics. The Union Jack stands proudly among them. In the center of the church, jutting out from the surrounding marble paving, is part of the original rock in the garden, and it's been preserved as the traditional spot where Jesus prayed.

The prayer commemorated by that rock is not what you or I normally associate with the word prayer: recollection, quiet, peace, calm, meditation. The New Testament uses the words: anguish, sweat, temptation, weakness, ignorance, uncertainty, silent tears.

I've always been grateful that this description of Jesus still exists in our records. I mean, there are other pages in the New

Testament which emphasize so strongly the extraordinary aspect of Jesus that you can begin to wonder, Is this person human? And indeed, people have actually suggested that Jesus didn't need to pray because he was God, and that when he did pray, he was only acting, to give us a good example. Well, this page of the New Testament reassures me! You don't act sweat, least of all a sweat of blood.

When Jesus had to take his own life into his hands, he wasn't posing for a stained glass window. He reacted as you or I would, with fear and trembling. And that's a great comfort to me. I find it difficult enough to call myself a follower of Jesus as it is. But if he had a whole lot of built-in advantages which I haven't got, and if he was happily screened off from all the built-in disadvantages which I have got, then I wouldn't know how to begin to be his follower.

This garden of Gethsemane assures me that Jesus had to live his life under the same conditions I live mine, in weakness and uncertainty, and that in the face of God's silence he remained true to God. So that here, as at Bethlehem, I'm glad to profess again my faith in man, especially in this man who shows me what I'm capable of, and reveals to me a God who loves me so much that he trusts me. It's God himself who says, in the life of Jesus, "I believe in Man."

HOLY SEPULCHRE

Pilate granted the corpse to Joseph who bought a shroud, took Jesus down from the cross, wrapped him in the shroud and laid him in a tomb which had been hewn out of the rock. He then rolled a stone against the entrance to the tomb. Mary of Magdala and Mary the mother of Joses were watching and took note of where he was laid.

When the Sabbath was over, Mary of Magdala, Mary the mother of James, and Salome, bought spices with which to go and anoint him. And very early in the morning on the first day of the week they went to the tomb, just as the sun was rising.

They had been saying to one another, "Who will roll away the stone for us from the entrance to the tomb?" But when they looked they could see that the stone, which was very big, had already been rolled back. On entering the tomb they saw a young man in a white robe seated on the right-hand side, and they were struck with amazement. But he said to them, "There is no need for alarm. You are looking for Jesus of Nazareth, who was crucified: he has risen, he is not here" (Mark 15:45–16:6).

For my last broadcast from Jerusalem, I've chosen the place which Christians first think of when you say the word Jerusalem, the place where Jesus was crucified, buried and raised to a new life by the power of God.

It's now called the church of the Holy Sepulchre. Once it was outside the city walls — because that's where they executed criminals — but now it's tightly wedged inside a Jerusalem which over the years has extended farther and farther beyond its original walls.

The various Christian communities who have staked out a claim here, each jealously guarding their little corner of the church — the western Christians represented by the Franciscan fathers in their characteristic brown habits, the Greek Orthodox with their flowing beards and flower-pot hats, the black-cowled Armenians and the turbaned Syrians, and the exotic negroid Abyssinians camped out on the roof — all these bear witness, by their very presence, to how sacred this spot has always been to Christians of every denomination.

It doesn't make life easy, this living in each other's pocket and breathing down each other's neck, and it tends to scandalize the newly arrived pilgrim. I remember vividly my first visit here, when I found the Greeks in their choir, and the Latins at the Sepulchre itself, and the Copts behind it, all holding a service at the same time, and at one point they were all singing and trying to shout each other down with same words, *Kyrie Eleison*; and I thought, "Lord have mercy!"

But on reflection I personally wouldn't have it otherwise. There's a great richness in this welter of rites and customs and traditions, all jostling with each other, and this would be sadly impoverished if they tidied it all up in the name of law and order. I would certainly miss the constant stream of disorganized Greek pilgrims who I now see in front of me, here at the foot of Calvary, where they venerate with great devotion the stone on which Jesus is said to have been anointed and prepared for burial. They know all about preparing people for burial — fathers and husbands and sons of theirs — these bent old Greek women.

What I find most moving about this building is the fact that it houses both Calvary and the Tomb. We haven't got two churches, one for Christ's death and one for his resurrection, only one. And this is a precious insight which Christians haven't always appreciated deeply enough, that these two events really are one. We mustn't think of the death of Jesus as if we could explain everything in terms of bloody sacrifices, and as if resurrection was added afterwards as a kind of unexpected bonus. More important still, we mustn't talk about the resurrection of Jesus as if it somehow neutralized or reversed his death. Jesus never recovers from his death. His resurrection is nothing other than that death seen with the eyes of God. Jesus died into that mystery that we call God, in such a way that his presence and his influence are no longer limited to the streets of Jerusalem or the lanes of Galilee. He lives on, and he is present, and he exercises his influence, wherever God is, which is everywhere.

I remember coming back to England from my first visit here, and a friend of mine asked me, 'How was it?" "Great," I said. "It's a wonderful thing to walk and touch and feel and see the country of Jesus." He said, "Did you discover that he's not there?"

The remark hasn't stopped me coming back here, many times, particularly to this place which reminds me of his death and resurrection. But it reminds me too — and I think we need reminding — that this isn't where I'm supposed to look for him. He is risen, and he stares at me out of the eyes of all those whom he called his "Body," which is all men, especially those who, like him, are in need.